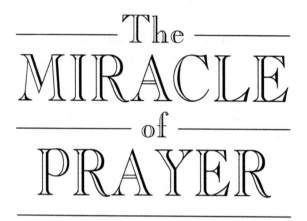

The MIRACLE of PRAYER

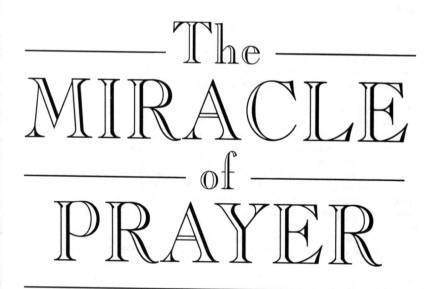

The MIRACLE of PRAYER

True Stories from
GUIDEPOSTS®
about the
Power of Prayer

TESTAMENT BOOKS
New York

Contents

Introduction

Finally, be strong in the Lord and in his mighty power.
. . . And pray in the Spirit on all occasions with all kinds
of prayer.

EPHESIANS 6 : 10, 18, NIV

There is no *one* way to pray. Our prayers and our praying
can be as individual as we are. But whether we write letters
to God, stand or kneel, pray out loud or silently, when we
pray we open ourselves up to God's presence in order to
receive His love and direction. So we must pray with joy,
knowing that God loves us and wants the best for us.

Praying is also taking time to listen for God to speak to
us and show us what we need to do, where we need to go.
And when we have gotten directions, then we obey. We
keep going even in the hard and difficult times. Because
prayer isn't a magic wand that instantly solves our problems. We must be persistent, both in praying and in doing
what God has given us to do.

Jesus taught us, "Whatever you ask in prayer, believing, you shall receive" (Matthew 21:22, RSV). So our

requests need to be specific, and, as you will discover, God delights in answering specific requests that we bring to Him in faith.

Although we may be convinced that prayer is a powerful force because we are praying to an Almighty God, sometimes praying is extremely difficult. Those are the times when it is necessary to give up our own ways, our own point of view, our own will, in order to enter the flow of God's blessing and power. When we have been wronged and are asked to forgive the one who wronged us, when we are shown our true selves and must acknowledge our weaknesses and failures to God, when we come to the end of our own power and ability and must surrender everything to God—at these times God asks of us nothing less than everything, our whole selves.

We do know that God promises to hear us when we pray. "Before they call, I will answer; and while they are yet speaking, I will hear" (Isaiah 65:24). Sometimes that may mean we get exactly what we pray for. But sometimes God gives us unexpected answers, surprises that show He loves us and knows what we need better than we do.

We invite you not only to read about prayer and what it accomplishes, but also to put into practice what you learn. Become a pray-er, an active part of the Guideposts family.

How To Pray

God be in my head
and in my understanding;
God be in my eyes
and in my looking;
God be in my mouth
and in my speaking;
God be in my heart
and in my thinking;
God be in my end
and in my departing.

FROM THE *OLD SARUM PRIMER* (1558)

How and When to Pray

THE EDITORS

No matter how, or when, or where we pray, God has promised to hear our prayers.

Jeremiah stood before God to pray for his people (Jeremiah 18:20)

Peter knelt to pray (Acts 9:40).

Nehemiah sat down when he prayed (Nehemiah 1:4).

Abraham prostrated himself while praying (Genesis 17:3).

Ezekiel prayed in a loud voice (Ezekiel 11:13).

Hannah prayed silently to the Lord (1 Samuel 1:13).

Paul prayed and sang in the spirit (1 Corinthians 14:15).

David prayed in the morning (Psalm 5:3).

Isaac prayed out in his field in the evening (Genesis 24:63).

Daniel prayed in his house three times a day (Daniel 6:10).

Anna prayed night and day in the temple (Luke 2:37).

For Scripture promises that "if we ask anything according to his will, he hears us. And...whatever we ask—we know that we have what we asked of him" (1 John 5:14–15, NIV).

Newfound Power in the Prayer Jesus Taught Us

ELAINE ST. JOHNS

One night several years ago a telephone call waked me out of a deep sleep. That was the night I began an adventure, a spiritual adventure, that goes on to this day. It involves a new, highly personal approach to the most beautiful, most familiar, most powerful prayer of all—the Lord's Prayer.

The call came about midnight. "I'm calling for Mona," said an unfamiliar voice. "Mona wanted me to tell you that Walt has had a massive heart attack. They're in an ambulance on their way to San Luis. Mona says, 'Pray for us.'"

Has it ever happened to you that, with a sudden shock, the well of prayer within you seems dry? It happened to me that night. I simply couldn't find words. All I could do was think of beautiful Mona, my closest spiritual friend, sitting beside the stricken form of her artist husband. I pictured the ambulance racing from their studio in the California coast village of Cambria to the city of San Luis Obispo thirty-five miles south.

"Pray for us," was Mona's message to me—but no prayer came.

"Help me to pray," I murmured to God. Quick as lightning some words flashed in my mind: *Pray the Lord's Prayer.* And like the echoing thunder my mind rejected them. "No use," I chided my subconscious. "I say the Lord's Prayer every day. It doesn't speak to the condition." Again the words came, more insistent, with additional emphasis: *PRAY the Lord's Prayer.*

Ah! That caught my attention. *Say* the Lord's Prayer. *Pray* the Lord's Prayer. Starting then I began to discover that there was a very real difference. That night I *prayed* His Prayer rather than simply repeating it like a child reciting the ABCs.

While I was praying, Mona and Walt were arriving at the hospital in San Luis. The prognosis for Walt was dire. Physicians, looking at a man past sixty who'd not only suffered a heart attack but had three clots in his lungs, pneumonia and a temperature of 107 degrees, believed he would not last the night.

But he did. And he lived for two years after that, fully active, then passed on quietly in his sleep. Those two years were a physical victory for Walt, but the telling point was spiritual. Walt had been a borderline agnostic. After that night, he and Mona at last shared spiritual treasure, for, she told me, "there was a complete change in his attitude toward God."

Was this coincidence or could it have been related to the power of the Lord's Prayer as I had prayed it? I had to believe the latter because, as I continued to pray it daily, the fruitage in my personal life was rich, satisfying, often unexpected. For example: An ugly tumor, scheduled for surgery, simply disappeared from my finger; it had been growing there since I slammed the finger in a car door. A financial crisis and a plaguey family squabble of some duration both evaporated without my taking thought. One afternoon when I picked up my granddaughter at school in answer to a "sick call," she was feverish, manifesting all the flu symptoms. While we drove I prayed as I was learning to do—and saw a normal child replace a sick one before my very eyes.

So how do you learn to pray the Lord's Prayer? Here are a few suggestions I offer from my own experience:

One. I found that it takes less than sixty seconds (even in church) to *say* the prayer, and anywhere from ten minutes to half an hour to *pray* it.

Two. There is no way to pray this prayer for one person or one family alone. The minute I consciously addressed "Our Father," even though my immediate concern was Walt and Mona, I was also including my family, friends, strangers, enemies—those who had "passed on" and those yet to arrive. I was praying for them as well. As I contemplated this I realized the universal intent of Christ when He gave the prayer to us.

Three. I had to be willing to be taught how to pray this prayer on a daily basis. I accepted the Holy Spirit as my guide and tried faithfully to follow the leadings that came to me. Some days I was moved to use the Bible concordance to gain understanding. In phrases like " Thy kingdom come, thy will be done," I looked up key words—*kingdom, will*— and meditated on what Jesus taught about them. Or I turned to the dictionary and looked up *forgive, debts, trespasses.* Sometimes I found myself simply praying it as a psalm of praise and adoration. But day by day, it yielded new insights.

Four. I came to recognize it as a complete prayer, nothing left out. In my newspaper days I was taught that a complete story answers the questions who, where, when, why, what. As I meditated on the Lord's Prayer, I found that it answers them all. And I found that it spoke to all conditions.

When we pray, "Thy kingdom come, thy will be done on earth as it is in heaven," we make supplication not only for our own known and unknown needs but also for the needs of His children everywhere. This, to me, was the source of those unexpected results in my own experience— the healing of my finger, my finances, my family relationships—without taking thought. The implications on a worldwide scale were overwhelming.

Five. There was something I had to do to become a clear channel for this power. "Forgive us...as we forgive...." Forgive meant to "give up resentment against or the desire to punish; to stop being angry with." Debtors were those who I felt "owed" me something, including certain behavior, such as respect, affection, gratitude. Trespassers had "wronged" me in some way, violated my territory, encroached, invaded. To my surprise I found those I felt had *wronged* me fewer than those who *owed* me, but it made me aware of what I considered trespasses. I came to believe that every time I made a judgment about someone, or criticized or just plain gossiped, I was trespassing.

So I made lists and worked diligently on all the aspects of forgiveness. It hasn't been quick or easy. In fact, I find I have to keep working at it. But with the doing has come great freedom—and peace, and the release of healing into all my relationships.

Six. I found I had to come to terms with the unexpected. Although I was learning alone, I rarely felt I was praying alone. At times I actually felt I was praying with the Master and His disciples in Galilee, and they were praying with me. Or I seemed to enter into the body of prayer, beyond or above time, so to speak, of which everyone who had ever prayed these words was still a part—and the sense of unity and power in that body of prayer was awesome.

Seven. As the prayer became part of my day's consciousness, there was a bonus of grace that continued after I had finished the actual praying; an aura of pleasure and peace clung to me hour by hour. It changed my days as dramatically as though a black-and-white world had been transformed into living color. If I was tempted to let it fade, something would surface to recall me.

One day, when I was caught in a crush at a department store sale, an unlikely recollection popped into my head: Chief Justice Oliver Wendell Holmes had once said that his whole religion could be summed up in the first two words of the Lord's Prayer. Fleetingly, as I dodged a flying elbow,

I wondered, *Why that thought now?* Of course! *Our Father.*
As I repeated it there, I saw that these unruly people were
His children, just as I was, and my panic subsided. I made
my way calm and unscathed to an exit. Or, when faced with
a personal crisis, I would find that magnificent affirmation
Thine is the kingdom and the power and the glory rising to
reassure me.

Less dramatically I found myself given a single word to
say over and over that seemed to keep the contact open. It
is a very old word, one used by Moses, by Jesus, by Paul,
by all Christians today. But it had been renewed for me by
my studies. It means "hearty agreement, steadfastness,
truthfulness." It means "So be it!...So it is." It is praise,
thanksgiving, blessing. Our Lord used it to close His
Prayer. I would like to use it now as a benediction for all of
us who attempt to *pray* His Prayer.

Amen.

Letters to God

Myrel Allison

My friend and I were both going through painful times. Joan (I've changed her name) was suffering in the aftermath of a child's death and I was torn up by the dissolution of a thirty-five-year marriage.

We were sitting on the glider on her screened-in porch and I'd been talking about the ups and downs of faith, how sometimes when you need God most, you feel most distant from Him. "Lately, I can't seem to concentrate on my prayers," I confessed. "I'm too scared and sorry for myself. I get caught up in feelings of unworthiness!"

A few minutes later, Joan excused herself to get iced tea for us. She came back with two tall glasses and a piece of paper with some closely written lines on it.

"Maybe you'll think I'm silly when you read this," she said, handing the sheet to me, "but I just started writing ... and so much came out!"

"Dear God," I read," things have been so unbearable in my life lately that sometimes I wonder if I'll ever feel like laughing again..."

What began as a letter of hurt and complaint to God, ended eventually as a beautiful prose-poem praising Him. In effect, Joan had found her own way to pray. "You have no idea how helpful writing that letter has been to me," she told me.

"Yes, I think I do," I replied. "And I think I know why you showed your 'prayer' to me."

Sure enough, when I myself began writing to God, putting my thoughts and feelings on paper, my feeling of intimacy with Him was strengthened. For five years I've been using this method of prayer, and I developed a guide-word to help me write my letters: ACTS. Perhaps you will find this guideword useful, too (it also comes in handy when I'm unexpectedly asked to pray in a group and my mind goes blank).

Adoration This is the salutation, in which you reverently acknowledge God's power, wisdom and love. It can be as simple as "Dear Heavenly Father" or as elaborate as you care to make it.

Confession You ask God's forgiveness for things you've neglected to do, for things you " know better than" but do anyway—for not showing love, not being forgiving, living life selfishly. Often my list is long.

Thanksgiving In this part, you can really wax poetic if you're so moved, thanking God for the gifts of nature, family, friends, health, freedom and, most of all, the gift of Jesus.

Supplication The asking, petitioning part. How consoling it is to turn my troubles, and those of others, over to God, to plead for His help and know He cares!

As I read back over my notebooks filled with prayer letters to God, I can see how I've grown, and how the Lord has been working in my life. Writing to Him helps me pull my thoughts together and keeps my mind from wandering.

Prayer letters. They're a literal way to worship God!

Free

No postage stamps for prayers we send,
    The mails do not affect them;
They go without a second's pause
    The moment we direct them.

MILDRED N. HOYER

The Prayer of Joy

CATHERINE MARSHALL

I know of a home in Washington, D.C., that used to be full of tension because of an aunt's nagging fault-finding with the children. The mother of the family did much praying about this situation—mostly that God would take away the aunt's hypercritical attitude. Nothing at all seemed to happen as a result, except that the mother's resentment of the aunt's attitude steadily increased.

One afternoon the mother—whom I had known for many years—dropped by my home to return a borrowed book.

"I know I must look a wreck," she apologized. "I feel like a ball knocked back and forth between the children and Auntie."

In the midst of discussing her problem, I had a sudden inspiration. "You've been asking God to change your aunt's disposition, and you say she's more fault-finding than ever. So why not forget about trying to change your aunt and make the burden of your prayer simply a request that everyone in your home have fun together?"

Immediately, she seemed challenged by this new idea. "It sounds almost too simple," she said, "but will you pray with me about it right now?"

As I recall, her prayer went something like this: "Lord, I know it's Your will that we have a happy household. But there has been no gladness in us. I ask that Your joy may flow full and free into our home. Help us and Auntie to have fun together; to find new ways of pleasing each other; to rediscover laughter. Amen."

A week later my friend telephoned. She said that day by day her prayer was being abundantly answered. "The atmosphere here at home is completely different. You know this joy business is dynamite! But I still don't understand why there's such power in it."

Perhaps one of the reasons that many of us do not understand the power of joy is that we have been wrong in thinking of Jesus Christ as primarily "a man of sorrows, and acquainted with grief" (Isaiah 53:3). No man with an attitude of gloom could ever have drawn little children to Him. Only a virile man who went out to meet life with unflagging zest could have attracted rugged fishermen as His disciples. Sadness couldn't last long when a man delightedly threw away his crutches or a leper went off leaping and singing on his way to show his clean new flesh to the priest.

Certainly He knew about life's problems and disappointments. "In the world ye shall have tribulation," He promised His disciples. "But," He added, "be of good cheer; I have overcome the world" (John 16:33).

Long before Jesus' day, many of the ancient Israelites had stumbled on the truth that God's love is closely akin to joy. "A merry heart doeth good like a medicine (Proverbs 17:22). "Serve the Lord with gladness: come before his presence with singing" (Psalm 100:2).

One of Webster's definitions of joy is that of an emotion excited by the "expectation of good." I wonder if this "expectation of good" does not represent an important approach to prayer? Certainly Agnes Sanford, the Episcopal rector's wife who has had much success with prayers for healing, tells story after story in her book *The Healing Light* to illustrate this.

She first met the power of joy when her own baby had been ill for six weeks with abscessed ears. Her prayers for healing, she said later, were negated by the fear and desperation in her heart. Then, one day, a young minister called.

"I'll go upstairs and have a prayer with the baby," he offered.

Mrs. Sanford was skeptical about his prayer achieving anything that her's had not, but showed him the way to the baby's room. She said later, remembering the incident, "Light shone in the minister's eyes. I looked at him and saw his loving joyfulness, and I believed. For joy is the heavenly 'okay' of the inner life of power."

The baby promptly went to sleep. When he awoke, he was well.

There was no aspect of gloom in the young minister even though the situation might have called for a somber manner. Thus it is quite possible to find the way to pray with joy in a very serious and seemingly tragic situation.

Do we need healing? One way is to ask ourselves why we want health. Then to make a series of happy pictures in our minds of the ways we would use health.

Do we need financial help? One way of joyous prayer is to create a series of pictures in the mind of the creative way in which we would use money.

Or do we want to love? The truth is that love and joy are inseparably connected. On the negative side, when we judge or are hypercritical, when we belittle or carp, love is nowhere in sight. On the positive side, love—to be love—must have joy in it; must have goodwill; must want the best for the beloved; must want to withhold no blessing—does not even ask whether the blessings are deserved or earned.

I had this connection between love and joy dramatized for me some years ago when a woman asked my advice about her marriage. She had just had the hardest blow any feminine ego can sustain: her husband had announced that he was going to leave her.

Mrs. B. was full of harsh criticism of her husband: he never went to church; he spent little time with their children; he was unfaithful. "Only God can change him," Mrs. B. intoned, gloomily.

Having seen by then many answers to prayer as the result of combining love with joy, I suggested to Mrs. B. that she demonstrate her love by asking God to rain His blessings—spiritual, physical, and material—on her husband, then leave him to God.

It turned out that she was unwilling to pray that way. "The only thing that will ever bring him to his senses and back to God is trouble and more trouble" was her view. And her prayers fell to the ground. The husband eventually got a divorce and married someone else.

I have often wondered what would have happened if my friend had prayed for her husband with a prayer of joy. She thought that she loved her husband. Yet, in God's eyes, real love is never just a reaction to another's behavior. Love itself takes joyous initiative in creative action.

Recently, I have been pondering this principle of the power of joy in relation to world peace. Even for those who completely believe in prayer, it isn't easy to know how to pray for other nations. It's especially hard when their ideals are not ours and when we are considered enemies.

But perhaps Christ is saying to us: "The people of all nations are My children. If you are going to be true sons of My Father, you are going to have to bless them that curse you, even pray for them that despitefully use you."

Now obviously we cannot bless and pray for people who despitefully use us, or with whom we are at odds, unless our prayer has that element of just plain goodwill that lies at the heart of joy and love.

So, it may be that if even a handful of Americans could pray with that kind of joy for the people of nations such as Russia and Cuba [or Libya or Iraq; eds.]—with the expectation of good, asking for God's all-abundant blessings on them in every sphere—tremendous results would be forth-coming.

God's way is to make "his sun to rise on the evil and on the good" (Matthew 5:45), and His sun of love plus joy is the only power in the universe capable of transforming peo-ple and situations—even international ones.

How to Deepen Your Prayer Life

L. DOYLE MASTERS

If you want to deepen your prayer life, study the prayer Jesus prayed in the garden of Gethsemane (Luke 22:39–46).

As a spiritual exercise—and before reading the listing below—take a sheet of paper and jot down how this passage applies to your life.

Here are seven steps to spiritual strength contained in Christ's Gethsemane experience:

Place. Have a regular place to pray where you can feel in tune with God. Jesus "came out, and went ... to the Mount of Olives" (Luke 22:39) (vs. 39; all quotations from the RSV).

Practice. Develop the regular practice of prayer. It really helps to have the habit. Jesus went, "as was his custom" (vs. 39).

Privacy. There are times for group prayer, but personal growth in prayer usually comes from being alone with God. Jesus "withdrew from them about a stone's throw" (vs. 41).

Posture. Pray in any position, but remember that kneeling to pray helps develop humility. Jesus " knelt down and prayed" (vs. 41).

Purpose. Forget self, seek God's will. Jesus prayed, "nevertheless not my will, but thine, be done" (vs 42).

Price. Be ready to pay the price. Real prayer is the process of emptying oneself of negatives so that God can come in with His positive good. "And being in an agony he prayed more earnestly; and his sweat became like great drops of blood falling down upon the ground" (vs. 44).

Power. Prayer brings special help and power from above. "There appeared to him an angel from heaven, strengthening him" (vs. 43).

PRAYER THAT LISTENS

I Was Silent

I was silent
  and I heard His voice.
I was silent
  and He heard mine.

JOAN BARLAND HENDERSON

One Life to Choose

MAXINE MONTGOMERY

I knew a lot about life on a farm by the time I was twelve, for I had spent two summers in the gaunt farmhouse of my sister Nadine—a place which smelled faintly of lye soap and smoked ham and had bees in the weatherboarding. I remember wading through dog fennel and sliding down a clay bank to the outhouse and mincing barefoot through hay-stubble carrying a burlap-wrapped jug of water to thirsty hay hands. I had smelled the fragrance of sweet clover. But I wasn't having any.

"This is not for me," I told myself. I didn't want a life like Nadine's. I didn't want to be a farmer's wife.

I wanted to be a missionary—carrying the Greatest Story to those who had not heard, teaching heathen children in a mud hut if need be. The very thought of Africa could quicken the ache in me. I rejoiced each day in my well-mapped life and resolutely repeated my early decision: I will be a missionary. Wherever God leads, I will go.

Life was pretty serene until at age nineteen I met Clifford. He came to church one day with another sister's friend. I stood on the brink of love unaware. Just one deep blue glance, and I was helpless, tripped up by my own heartstrings. *Oh, let him be a preacher, Lord!*

When I heard him sing, I was lost. "God, do something," I pleaded. "Surely this is the one You have in mind for me."

But Clifford was a farmer. And that was exactly what he wanted to be. I sounded him out carefully, sure that God or someone had made a mistake.

No, he liked to farm. His hands fitted the steering wheel of a tractor. Nothing on earth gave him a greater sense of accomplishment than seeing the earth curling black behind his plow.

Still I baited him. "Cliff," I said, "there are other lands— a hundred mountains to climb, a desert to cross, new fields to cultivate...."

"I like it here," he said and kissed me squarely on the nose. "But I guess you're just not the type to carry an egg bucket."

Nothing changed during the next three years while I was teaching and going to college. Cliff wanted me to marry him—and I wanted to—but couldn't.

Yet all the time, he was indoctrinating me in the lore of the farm, and there came a summer day following my third year of college when my defenses caved in. It was the day I rode with him on the little Farmall while he mowed the clover meadow. I watched the swallows circling the field for the bugs aroused by his machine, and I thought I would drown in the purpling twilight. I was visualizing myself with a baby in my arms running to greet him at the end of a day like this.

"I'll marry you, Clifford," I said that night. We had taken our soda pop out beneath the maple tree and sat gazing at the moon floating in the pond below us.

I could hear the crickets begin to sing, and then the frogs took up the rhythm. I thought he would reach out for me, but he didn't. He sat silent with his back against the tree so long I thought that perhaps he had not heard.

"Cliff," I whispered. He grasped my hand, then lifted my chin tenderly. "You know it wouldn't work," he said at last. "You don't belong on a farm."

"I won't be unhappy," I argued. "I've made up my mind."

But he shook his head. "You have to do what the Lord tells you to do. I would never forgive myself if you missed your way because of me."

"I know what I'm doing," I cried desperately, but he stood me on my feet and began walking me toward his car. And I knew he was right. How could I say to God that I wanted to go my own way?

"Lord," I cried all that night, "help me! Help me! Surely You have seen the pain in Clifford and You know the torment I have brought him. I am no longer sure of the way I should go. Lead me."

And I know that He did lead me. I had to go to the seminary; of that I was sure. I had to know beyond a shadow of doubt what God's will was for me. So I applied for a scholar-ship, and when it came, I said good-bye to Cliff—maybe, I thought, forever.

I plunged into seminary life with all the fervor and ener-gy I possessed. I took over a Sunday school department in one church and a training course in another. I gulped down great quantities of Old and New Testament.

Then I began to look about me. Surely God had some-one ready for me here. Maybe He had been leading me to the perfect mate all along. So I looked those preacher boys over. They were there by the hundreds. They laughed and talked and sang and preached on street corners on Friday nights and in churches on weekends. They were hand-some, gifted, warm-hearted. They were my dear friends, but none of them was especially for me.

Then another thought gripped me: maybe God expect-ed me to go it alone! The thought sent a deep pain through me—yet if that's what He wanted, I would go alone.

But one evening my best friend, Antonina, got me talk-ing about Cliff. She must have seen the loneliness in my eyes, and I'm sure it showed. I kept seeing Clifford driving his tractor, the swallows circling it. Anyway, in the course of our conversation, she challenged my commitment. "Maybe the Lord really has something else in mind for you. Have you asked Him lately?"

"I've pounded on His door every night!" I cried.

"And have you listened for the answer? Maybe you should just relax and wait."

"Relax?" I squeaked. And then we both laughed, for suddenly I saw myself slashing my way through underbrush when all I needed to do was to walk down the open pathway.

So I began to pray, not trying to convince God that I was right, just praying quietly and in deep faith. I knew He was my loving Father. I knew He did indeed have my life plan marked out. If Clifford and his farm were a part of it, He surely would let me know.

One day when I was sick with the flu, the answer came. I had prayed joyfully, knowing that the answer was there already in the heart of God. Then I slept; and as I slept, a voice spoke softly. I turned and saw Clifford's face smiling at me and then I felt as if God were smiling on us both. Suddenly I sat up in bed. The answer was as clear as a cloudless Tuesday morning. "Yes, I must marry Cliff," I said aloud.

"The answer was there all the time," I wrote to Cliff. "All I had to do was trust God and look."

In the spring I became a farmer's wife and stood on our hilltop each morning watching Clifford's tractor and the sun rising through mists above purple hills.

It is still like that, and love an ever-new mystery to both of us. And God is here—in the turn of plow and the hum of the combine and the rattle of the hay elevator. I have watched Him walk among the sheep and cattle and laugh with our children.

Clifford and I witness together to His guiding power in

our local church, and now that our children are stretching into lives of their own, I am once more a schoolteacher. "Wherever He leads me," I am still saying, and keep bumping my head on the infinite.

"What Is It You're Looking For, Captain?"

THEODORE J. THIBEAULT

When you find yourself doing a bunch of oddball things that wind up making perfect sense, you can be sure God is at work. That's what I think today. Yet back in 1986, when the peculiarities began, I had no interest in God, nor did I ever dream that God might interest Himself in me—an old barnacle of seventy, with forty years in the merchant marine behind me.

Still, who else would put the idea of taking karate lessons into my head? Karate! I hadn't thought about it since I'd taken a few lessons in a class with my young son. But that was twenty-five years ago. Now I was entering my eighth decade. Healthy, except for some deafness. Happily married. Taking care of a cat and five dogs and tending an A-to-Z vegetable garden outside of Beaumont, Texas. Why were karate lessons on my mind? That was strange enough, but I also found myself thinking about the karate teacher my son and I had gone to: Charles Brocato.

I reached for the area phone directory and began leafing through it, thinking, *He's probably not in business anymore.* But I was wrong. When I dialed the number for Beaumont Karate and Judo Studio, Brocato himself answered.

"Do you have any age limits for karate?" I asked.

"We certainly do," he said.

That seemed to close the door for me, but I went on talking, telling him that I'd once studied with him briefly. He actually remembered me. "The unsinkable Captain Thibeault with all the World War II stories? No age limit for you," he said. "Come in and see me."

The day of my interview, I sat down in front of his desk with the oddest feeling, as if I'd come home. Odder things were about to happen.

Mr. Brocato looked me over. "I'm as strict as ever, Captain Thibeault."

I thought he was worried about my age and physical condition, so I thumped on my chest and said, "I'm in as good shape as I was twenty-five years ago. Better!"

"What is it you're looking for, Captain?"

"I guess I want to train toward my black belt," I told him lamely. To wear the black belt means you have attained the highest level of karate expertise.

Then he said the last thing I expected to hear. "Captain Thibeault, you think you want karate, but people who come to this studio now are sent here by God."

God? I blinked a couple of times. I hadn't thought about God since I'd gone off to sea as a teenager. Not even having three ships sunk under me in World War II had brought me back to the religion I'd grown up with in a devout French-Canadian family. God just wasn't real to me.

But apparently God was real to Mr. Brocato, and I didn't want to offend him. "If God sent me here, then what did He send me here for?" I asked.

"I teach Christian meditation along with the martial arts," Mr. Brocato replied. "I don't ask that you believe a word I say, I just want you to try it. If you do that, you'll find out what God wants of you."

I'm five feet three, and I wasn't about to argue with six feet of confidence and conviction. "I'll try it, "I promised.

"If you don't want to hear about Christ," he warned, "don't come into this studio. You will only be miserable."

"I haven't been to church in forty years, but I don't mind hearing about Christ. I'm ready to learn anything you want to teach me, sir."

He laughed and said, "Be here on Tuesday night with a permission slip from your doctor."

I was. And sure enough, as Mr. Brocato taught us beginning karate techniques—how to stand, how to make a proper fist—he began talking to us about Christ's teaching: living free of hate, fear and self-importance. As we studied kicks and blocks, we also practiced relaxation techniques that would prepare us for meditation, which Mr. Brocato defined as "listening for God to speak to us." While we learned to translate karate motions into the harmonious for-mal movements called *katas,* Mr. Brocato was encouraging us to buy and read a Bible and to learn about Christ.

One day after a hard workout, he really surprised me. He said, " Now, gentlemen, I want to speak to you about something we all need in order to prepare for meditation. I want you all to start praying."

This class of men—young, middle-aged and me—looked at one another.

"Don't worry. I'm going to make it easy for you. If you don't have anything or anyone to pray for, pray for me. I need your prayers so I can help you better."

I was dumbfounded. Mr. Brocato is the holder of black belts in karate, judo and jujitsu. He had been an intercollegiate wrestling champion and a professional wrestler. He had college degrees in biology and mathematics. And here he was, humbly asking for prayer!

So the first prayer I uttered since my childhood was a prayer for my karate instructor. Every day I went into my den and read the Bible. I prayed and tried to meditate. That was how much respect I had for Mr. Brocato and *his* faith. But I couldn't see what it had to do with me.

I had been praying for a month or two when the savings-and-loan association that held part of my life savings went bankrupt because of poor management. I stormed around the house ranting and raving. My wife, Doris, tried to soothe me, fearing I'd rush down to the bank and start a fight. When karate night rolled around, I felt so low I almost didn't go.

Mr. Brocato noticed my mood as I entered. He took me into his office and listened as I poured out the whole story. "I didn't want to come tonight," I said, "but something *told* me to come."

Mr. Brocato nodded. "Are you starving?" he asked calmly.

"No, but I'm seventy years old. I'll never be able to make that money back."

"Well, do you have any big bills?"

"No, my house is paid for, and I have Social Security and my seaman's pension. I don't owe any bills."

"Is your wife causing you any problems about this?"

"My wife? She's been wonderful! She's worried sick that I'm going to do something rash."

"Well, then, Captain Thibeault, you're looking at this all wrong," Mr. Brocato said. "You aren't starving, your wife loves you, your bills are paid, you like this studio, and you have a new interest and new friends, and you're learning about God. You're blessed."

"But they stole from me and they're getting away with it."

Mr. Brocato said, "That's between them and God. Your problem is that God has literally had His hand on your shoulder all your life, loving you and taking care of you. And you don't seem to realize it."

I thought about what Mr. Brocato said all during the karate workout that night, and I felt better.

Then came bad news. During a medical checkup, my doctor found I had Paget's disease, an affliction of the bones

mostly in older people, which in my case was causing mal-
formation of the skull bones. The thought of deformity was
depressing enough, but the real blow was what the doctor
told me about my hearing. "Start learning sign language
now," he said, "or learn to read lips. In a year, you'll be completely deaf."

I was too shocked to move or speak. The idea of total
deafness terrified me! Once again my troubled thoughts
turned to a familiar beacon—Mr. Brocato. I couldn't wait to
see him and tell him how frightened I was.

"What should I do?" I asked after I'd given him the
details.

He sat there a minute and looked me over. "Haven't you
heard one thing I've said in class?"

I had no idea how his lectures in class applied to the
fact that I was about to go deaf, but I said quickly, "Yes, sir!
I've done everything you said."

He seemed exasperated with me. "Well, then," he said,
"did you take it to Jesus?"

This made even less sense to me. "How, sir?"

Mr. Brocato saw that I was so beside myself, so fas-
tened upon the idea of deafness-in-a-year, that I couldn't
understand anything unless he explained it very carefully.
He began, " Do you remember how I taught you to pray and
to meditate?"

"Yes, sir! I work on it every day."

"Then take it to Jesus in prayer," he said.

I was so rattled I couldn't think. "What should I say to
Him?" I asked.

He looked at me again and shook his head. "Say this: 'Jesus, my instructor said I have the right to come before You and ask You for help. Because You died for me. I don't want to be deaf, Jesus. Is there anything I can do to avoid it?' Then meditate. You will get an answer. *Believe!* He *will* answer you."

I looked at this man whose belief was so strong, and suddenly, as if a spark leapt between us, that same belief was humming inside *me* like electricity. *God is real. He cares about me.*

I jumped up. I said, "I believe! If you say it's so, I believe it." And I did. Totally. With every fiber.

At home, I went to my den, read my Bible and prayed. "Jesus, my instructor said it was all right for me to ask You what to do. I don't want to be deaf. Please tell me what I can do." I emptied my mind and listened the way I had been taught.

The answer was unlike anything I had ever experienced before. It was a voice, yet not a voice, and it broke over me like a wave: *Go back to your doctor.*

I sprang to my feet in excitement. I believed without the slightest doubt Jesus had answered my prayer. Immediately I called my doctor's secretary for an appointment.

The doctor was surprised to see me. "I already told you," he said. " There is nothing more I can do. Learn sign language now. In a year, you will be deaf."

I argued with him. I was convinced he had something that would help me, even if he didn't know what it was.

After ten minutes of my arguing and his denying it, however, I started out the door.

My hand was on the knob when the doctor suddenly said, "Oh, by the way...." He looked at me strangely. "Something did come across my desk this morning." He hunted through papers. "Ah! Here it is. A new procedure is being used in cases like yours. This is about a doctor nearby who is doing it."

I knew my hearing was saved.

The new doctor, Dr. Boyd Herndon, checked me. He said I was a good candidate for surgery and he would operate on my bad ear. But he warned me that I could become totally deaf in that ear, that I could be left paralyzed on the left side of my face, and that I could lose my sense of taste.

I paid no attention. "Let's get on with it," I said.

Doris was frightened by the mention of paralysis. "Wait a minute," she said. "Let's think about this."

"God is going to restore my hearing," I told her. "After His answer I'd be a fool to doubt."

When the bandages were finally being taken off, Dr. Herndon said, "After I get the cotton out of your ear, we will test it to see how much hearing you have."

"Doctor," I said, "you don't need to test it. I can hear you right now through the cotton."

Dr. Herndon shook his head. He hurried to remove the cotton. He had me close off my good ear so that he could test the ear he had operated on. I had better hearing in my formerly bad ear than in my good ear!

What amazed my doctors and my wife more than the success of the operation was my unwavering faith that my ear was already saved. I believed Jesus had answered me. I didn't care about warnings of side effects, no matter how dire.

Now I knew why God had sent me to Mr. Brocato: so his conviction could kindle mine. So I could obey the first great commandment: "Thou shalt love the Lord thy God with all thy heart, and with all thy soul, and with all thy mind" (Matthew 22:37).

And I do.

The Listening Ear

Be still and know
That God is in His world.
God speaks, but none may hear
That voice except he have
The listening ear.

AUTHOR UNKNOWN

PRAYER AND THE FAMILY

When Father Prays

When father prays the house is still,
his voice is slow and deep.
We shut our eyes, the clock ticks loud;
so quiet we must keep.

Sometimes the prayer gets very long
and hard to understand,
and then I wiggle up quite close,
and let him hold my hand.

I can't remember all of it,
I'm little yet, you see;
but one thing I cannot forget,
my father prays for me.

AUTHOR UNKNOWN

The Comfort of Prayer

CHARLES R. HOLLIS

Mother and Dad's fiftieth wedding anniversary was marred by Dad's health—recently he had suffered a heart attack and we feared another. That night, upstairs in my room in their farmhouse, I worried about my folks.

Life had often been difficult for them. Of five sons and one daughter, two sons were lost in the war; a third returned to them a casualty. Their love helped him to recover.

"Why more sickness and trouble for them when they've spent their lives doing so much for others?" I asked myself now.

Suddenly I heard voices downstairs. It was late and the sounds—though soft—startled me. Perhaps Dad had had another attack.

I got out of bed and hurried down the stairs to see if I were needed.

Halfway down I stopped. The soft murmur was distinct now and I could hear the words:

"Thy kingdom come, Thy will be done ..." Mother and Dad were repeating the Lord's Prayer.

Leaning over the bannister, I could see Dad sitting in his chair with Mother kneeling beside him, her hands lightly placed on top of his as if enveloping him in love. I couldn't see Mother's face but Dad looked peaceful and content as he said the words.

I stood still for a second or two and then turned quietly and went back to my room.

It was more than an act of faith—their prayer gave me understanding that replaced fears and questions. Later I was able to cope with illness and discouragement by the memory of that night.

Mother and Dad had not been troubled. They still had God's Presence to comfort and sustain them, just as they had had all their fifty years together.

Picnic Pick-Me-Up
Priscilla Davis

My husband, Gary, an electrician, had been laid off from his job. Less than a week later, things became even bleaker when he fell through a cattle guard and crushed his leg. He'd be hobbled for several months.

In time I found a job feeding and watering eight thousand chickens. As Gary recovered and didn't need his crutches anymore, he got a job spraying herbicides on farmers' fields. But even though we were both working and meeting our bills, Gary couldn't shake his depression. He brooded; supper became a silent time. I felt empty and went so far as wondering if I should have married him.

A month passed, and I constantly begged God to change Gary. I wondered, though, if God could reach my husband, a man who'd never had much patience for talk of faith. In any case, there seemed nothing I could do. And then one morning, as I knelt to dust the coffee table, I heard a still voice saying, *Priscilla, do you want this marriage to work? Well, then, get up. Go fix Gary a picnic lunch and find him in the field.*

I packed a large woven basket full of Gary's favorite foods. Our three-year-old son, Christopher, and I hopped into the car, then went bumping along the rough back roads. We spotted Gary and waved. Gary swung the tractor around, struggled to get off and then limped toward us, a big grin already spreading across his face.

Where would we picnic? "There's a little shaded churchyard down the road," Gary said. "Why don't we go there?"

We came to a country church, sitting atop a little knoll. We ate our lunch under a big ash tree. We talked and laughed as our small son climbed on the churchyard stones. After the meal we quietly peeked inside the church. It was musty smelling but peaceful—a peace that I watched take hold of Gary.

For the next month God showed me new ways of caring for my husband: a simple squeeze of the hand, helping in the fields so that Gary wouldn't have to get off the tractor to fill the spraying tanks.

Fall came. Gary was called back to his electrician's job, and it was there that a man shared the gospel with him. I'll never forget the evening Gary rushed home, dropped his lunch box on the counter, found my Bible and began to read.

He hasn't stopped since, and our family has undergone a deep change. All for the better. And where did the change begin? Not in Gary, as I had prayed. No, God in His wisdom answered my prayer by changing *me* first.

From now on I hope I'll know better. Whenever I want someone else to change, I'll stop and say, "Tell me, Lord, should the change really begin with me?" Yes will be the most likely answer.

The Coffeepot Experiment

CATHERINE MARSHALL

The scene is forever etched in my memory. It was a winter evening, 1959, soon after after my marriage (after ten years of widowhood) to Leonard LeSourd. The setting was our new home in Chappaqua, New York, a sprawling white house with red shutters. We were gathered around the dinner table for our first meal as a new family with Len's three children: Linda, age ten; Chester, six; Jeffrey, three. My son, Peter, nineteen, was away at Yale University.

I had lovingly prepared food I thought the children would enjoy—meat loaf, scalloped potatoes, broccoli, a green salad. Len's face was alive with happiness as he blessed the food.

But then as Chester's big brown eyes regarded the food on his plate, he grimaced, suddenly bolted from the table, fled upstairs and refused to return.

"Let him go, Catherine," Len said. Then, seeing the stricken look on my face, he explained ruefully, "I'm afraid my children are not used to much variety in food. Mostly

I've just fed them hamburgers, hot dogs, or fried chicken from a take-out place."

Had Len and I but known, that disastrous scene was but a foretaste of what lay ahead. Linda's hostility toward her new stepmother was all too apparent. The two boys wanted to room together, yet were forever fighting like bear cubs. One night when they started scrapping again, Len summarily removed Jeff to another room. The little guy sobbed himself to sleep.

Later on that same night after Len and I, exhausted, had just fallen asleep, the shrill ringing of the telephone awoke us. It was Peter. "Mom, I got picked up for speeding on the Merritt Parkway. I'm at the police station." We agreed to post bond for Peter's release.

Yet all these troubles were but surface symptoms, the tip of the iceberg of difficulties. Flooding in on us day after day were the problems of parents and relatives, together with the children's emotional trauma from six housekeepers in ten months. Even Peter was still suffering from the loss and shock he received as a nine-year-old when his father, Peter Marshall, died.

How do you put families broken by death or divorce back together again? How can a group of individuals of diverse backgrounds, life experiences and ages ever become a family at all? I knew I didn't have all the answers, but I also knew Someone who did.

So I began slipping out of the bedroom early while the children were still asleep for a quiet time of talking-things-over prayers, Bible reading and writing down thoughts in my *Journal*.

During those early morning times slowly there dawned the realization of something I had not wanted to face: Len was one of those men who felt that his wife was more "spiritual" than he, somehow had more Christian know-how. Len liked to point out that I was more articulate in prayer. Therefore, he was assuming that I would take charge of spiritual matters in our home while he would handle disciplining the children, finances, etc.

I already knew how many, many women there are who find it difficult to talk with their husbands about religion, much less pray with them. How could I make Len see that "spirituality" was as much his responsibility as mine? "Lord, what do I do about this one?" I hurled heavenward.

Somehow the answer was given me that nagging a male about this would not work. My directive was to go on morning by morning with the quiet time, but otherwise refuse to accept that spiritual responsibility for the home. The assurance was given me that God would work it out.

After a few more days, Len became curious about why I was getting up early. Persistently he questioned, "What are you *doing* each morning?"

"Seeking God's answers for my day. I know He has them, but I have to ask Him, then give Him the chance to feed back to me His guidance. You see, if I don't take time for this as the kickoff of the day, it gets crowded out."

"That would be good for me, too," was Len's reaction. "After all, we're in this together. Why not set the alarm for fifteen minutes earlier and pray together before we start the day?"

Thus an experiment began that was to change both our lives. The next day at a local hardware store I found an electric timer to plug into our small four-cup coffeepot. That night I prepared the coffee tray at bedtime and carried it to the bedroom. The following morning we were wakened by the pleasant aroma of coffee rather than an alarm clock going off.

We drank our coffee, and I started to read at a spot in Philippians. But Len wanted to get on with the prayer. "You start, Catherine," he said sleepily.

"But how are we going to pray about this problem of Linda's lack of motivation to study?" I asked. A discussion began. It got so intense that time ran out before we got to actual prayer.

Len agreed that we needed more time. Our wake-up hour went from 6:45 to 6:30 to 6:00. Discipline in the morning meant going to bed earlier. It became a matter of priorities. The morning time together soon changed from an experiment to a prayer-shared adventure.

By this time, Len, always methodical, had purchased himself a small five-by-seven, brown loose-leaf notebook. He began jotting down the prayer requests, listing them by date. When the answers came, those too were recorded, also by date, together with how God had chosen to fill that particular need. Rapidly, the notebook was becoming a real prayer log.

Not only that, as husband and wife, we had found a
great way of communication. Bedtime, we already knew,
was a dangerous time to present controversial matters to
one another. When we were fatigued from the wear and
pressures of the day, disagreements could erupt easily.

Yet when we tackled these same topics the next morning in an atmosphere of prayer, simply asking God for His
wisdom about it, controversy dissolved and communication
flowed easily.

Perhaps an actual page out of the brown notebook best
tells the story....

Prayer Requests—
December 15, 1959

1. That we find household help so that Catherine can con-
    tinue writing *Christy*.
2. That Peter will do more work and less playing around
    at Yale.
3. That Linda will be more motivated in her studies.
4. That Chester will stop fighting with his brother and
    accept his new home situation.
5. That we can find the way to get Jeff toilet-trained.

Morning by morning, the requests piled up and up...
Linda's rebelliousness; a personnel problem at Len's office
in New York; a friend with cancer; guidance as to which
church to attend; a relative with a drinking problem; very

close friends with difficulties with their children—and on and on.

We were learning more about prayer: that specific requests yield precise answers. So we did not simply ask for household help, we recorded a request for live-in help, a good cook, someone who loved children, who would be warm and comfortable to live with.

The day came when Len set down the answer to this in the brown notebook—middle-aged Lucy Arsenault. She was sent through Len's mother who had known her in Boston years before. Finding her enabled me to resume writing *Christy.*

The answer to Jeff's little problem came through the homely advice of the country general practitioner near the farm in Virginia. Irrepressible Jeff was simply too lazy to get up and go to the bathroom, too well-padded with too many diapers. Waterproof the bed, take all diapers off, let him wallow in wet misery. It worked—miraculously.

Now unless we had been recording both the request and the answer, with dates, we might have assumed these "coincidence" or just something that would have happened anyway. But with those written notations marking the answers to prayer, we found our gratitude to God mounting. The prayer log was a marvelous stimulus to faith.

Not that everything always worked out the way we wanted. We found that prayer is not handing God a want-list and then having beautiful answers float down on rosy clouds. God seemed especially interested in our learning patience and to trust *Him,* rather than man's manipulative devices for answers. Also, His timing is certainly not ours. Most answers came more slowly than we wished, and piecemeal. There continued to be some health problems. Two Marshall grandchildren died soon after birth. I worked for two years on a book I finally had to abandon. It took twelve years of anguish and many different kinds of prayer before Linda's life was turned around. But the turning point came with beautiful timing.

One of the best answers of those early days was Len's dawning realization that unless he became the spiritual head of our home, Chester and Jeffrey would grow up considering religion as something for the womenfolk. He had always considered his prayers too "bread and potatoes." But the boys liked that. So, as Len continued to say grace and lead the family prayer time, the boys began praying too—as if it were the natural thing to do.

Thus our husband-wife morning prayer time has set the tone and direction for twenty years of marriage.* That original coffee-timer (still operating although with many new parts) is one of our most cherished possessions. We know that neither one of us, or both of us, without God, have the wisdom to handle the problems which life hands us day by day. But as early morning prayer partners we have added assurance that " where two or three are gathered together" in His name, God is indeed with us. We know that communication between us, and between us and our children, has opened up. We can be sure that our morning prayers to

*Written in 1979.

God have mutual support and we know, from our prayer log, that those prayers are answered.

Why don't you go out and buy yourself a coffeepot and a timer? Try awakening to the pleasant aroma of coffee. Try approaching the problems of the day, partnered in prayer and with a fresh mind, and you may find—as Len and I have—a lifeline to cling to all day long.

How to Handle a Hard Day

RUTH WARD

Despite the hustle and bustle of a hectic world, our family has found a new way to make prayer part of our daily lives.

In our designated places at the dining table, each person prays for the person on his right every day for a week. The next week we switch to the person on our left and then the one directly across the table. Each shares particular needs of the day with the one praying for him. We also ask each family member to pick out his or her hardest day of the week. That day becomes the one when everyone prays especially for that person and his or her name is posted on the refrigerator as a reminder to all of us.

Kay, a senior in high school, chose Monday as her day because it's packed full with piano-practicing beginning at 5:30 a.m., then classes, homework and teaching piano students after dinner. Her day ends with youth choir rehearsals. She needs patience and concentration to get through it all.

On Tuesday, surprise solos are regularly on the agenda of the sixth-grade band, so Roger chose that day to let prayers bolster his courage.

Wednesday is Julia Beth's day because ninth-graders have all their major subjects on that day and she comes home weighted down with homework.

David, an eleventh grader, needs special understanding and patience on Thursdays when he makes his paper-route collections—whatever the weather.

Friday is Mother's day because after substitute-teaching all week, fulfilling the duties of a minister's wife and trying to keep straight a house that's becoming increasingly more cluttered, I need help to keep calm and organized.

Dad's day falls on Saturday when he needs special wisdom as he makes final sermon preparations and personal visits. Since there are only six members in our family, we award Daddy the extra day on Sunday because he needs special insight for his work at church that day.

One Friday, when the flu caused me to miss preparing breakfast and seeing the children off to school, I was gratified to find my name posted on the refrigerator as I was getting juice. If I fail to post a name, someone else usually does it.

But even the smoothest systems sometimes break down. At the end of one Wednesday, Julia Beth asked dejectedly, "Did anyone pray for me today? I didn't feel like anyone did."

Sure enough, her suspicions were confirmed—we all had failed her. We had forgotten to post her name and overlooked her in our special prayers.

Since then we have become more aware than ever of one another's needs and more concerned for each individual's problems. But most important, we are learning as a family the true power of prayer, believing in it now even more as it helps each one of us cope with whatever each new day brings.

Our Prayer Bulletin Board

MICHELLE C. HOLMES

The first thing I noticed when I entered the kitchen this morning was the sign on our bulletin board: one word in big, bold letters—PATIENCE. And I recalled that I'd put it there myself—just last night—because patience is something I need in my chaotic life right now.

Our family uses this kitchen bulletin board as a sort of central prayer-request board. In the past we've posted a photo of a starving child in Ethiopia (to remember to pray about the famine), a yellow ribbon (to remind us of the hostages), a picture of a special aunt (to think of her as she undergoes surgery).

Then, each night when we have grace before our evening meal, we can look at these mementoes and visualize who and what we are praying for.

"Pray one for another," the Bible tells us (James 5:16). In our busy lives, our family's "prayer pics" board helps us to do just that—and more.

Children of Pain

IKE KEAY

Today I work in a home for children, the only one of its kind in the country. It's a home for children whose parents are in prison. Many of these little ones have lived through cursings, beatings and broken bones. Some have even seen one parent murder the other. When they come to us, they don't know much about tenderness, about hugging. They do know about rejection and abuse. And guilt. And shame.

Here at Bethel Bible Village we give them love, warmth and a caring family atmosphere. We don't have dormitories, we have homes. But even when the children leave us, there's something else I can give them, something I discovered many years ago.

It seems so strange how all this has come about, that I should be the one responsible for these children. Though my life began differently, we ended up having a lot in common.

My younger brother and I were born in Scotland to the son of a successful dairyman and to a sensitive young woman whose parents had emigrated to America. Father was robust and hard-working; a good businessman and sportsman. My mother, Johanna Christina Keay, was gentle, delicate of health but strong of spirit, always ready to ease us through difficult times. I vaguely remember one of the most heartbreaking times for her. It was 1937, when I was five, and my brother, three.

We were waiting for Father to come home from work, when Mother took us gently into her arms to break the news: "Dears, your father has been in a hunting accident. ... He'll never be coming home again. He's dead, and I think we must make a fresh start. So, I'm going to take you both to America to live with my parents, in New Jersey."

A few weeks later, we waved good-bye to Grandpa and Grandma, to the farm, and boarded a ship for America. Life there was rough. We lived in Newark, New Jersey. Mother's parents were not prosperous and were unprepared for the energies and antics of two young boys. Mother worked six days a week, while we stayed with our grandparents.

We had no money, but on Sundays, after church, Mother walked with us through a nearby cemetery, the most beautiful spot in our neighborhood. We played games and sang and daydreamed together. And while my brother and I snuggled in the curve of her arms, she read to us, often from the Bible.

Then, after four years in America, tragedy struck again: Mother developed tuberculosis, a disease that had already wiped out much of her family. "Please, *ple-e-ase,* let us stay with you, Mother!" I had begged over and over. "Please don't send us away!"

Three days later, her brother drove us to a children's home, and we cried all the way. Then we wept more bitterly, as we saw our mother ride away, leaving us with strangers. Little did we realize that she was going into a sanatorium and was not expected to live.

The home was on a farm of 212 acres overlooking a river and a swamp. I saw the large dormitories—each housing twenty-one homeless kids—through a blur of tears.

I was taken to my dorm in a state of bewilderment and shock. *Oh, God, what is happening? Where is my mother?*

Finally that terrible first day ended, darkness came; mercifully, sleep ended my nightmare. But this brief escape came to an abrupt end as I heard a harsh voice barking, "Hey, kid! Get out of that bed! It's time to get up."

"What?...Who?" I asked drowsily.

"Yeah, *you,* Buck Teeth," yelled the gruff voice. "It's six-fifteen; that's when we get up here."

That was my introduction to the older guys. Because my buck teeth stuck out like a woodchuck's, I was called Woodchuck, or Beaver, or The Plow, for many of the years I lived at Glengary (not the school's real name).

The next day I was stopped by Mom Patterson, a small, stern woman, over sixty-five—so unlike my own mother—with a rasping voice: "Keay, did you see those boys smoking in the locker room?"

Mother had always taught us to be truthful, and so I naively admitted: "Yes, ma'am, they were smoking."

Later that evening the boys were waiting for me in the locker room. "So you're a squealer, huh? We're gonna teach you a lesson!" One of them twisted my arms behind my back, and the other guys began punching me. My knees buckled from fright and I cried out in pain. They only laughed and beat me all the more.

"We'll show you what happens to squealers, Buck Teeth," growled one.

"Oh, yes, I saw 'em smokin'," mimicked another in a high voice as he yanked my hair and pushed me against the wall.

When they had finished with me, they threw me on the floor. Once again I cried myself to sleep.

One morning I discovered I had wet my bed. The older boys found out and made fun of me. They made me take an ice-cold shower.

For days and weeks and months, it seemed *forever*, it was the same—the older boys bullying the younger ones.

I had never known such cruel treatment before, and I longed for Mother to come and rescue my brother and me.

"Stop that crying, you little sissy!" the boys would tell me. Then they'd beat me some more, to make me tough, they said.

When I'd receive a letter from Mother, I'd feel loved again. She wrote to my brother and me faithfully, twice a week. Sometimes about the scenes from her window; sometimes about our father, whom we wanted to emulate because Mother described his attributes.

At Glengary, every child had chores before and after school and on Saturday mornings. Either carpentry and maintenance or gardening or husbandry. We raised our own food and did all the cleaning and repairs. It was hard; but it was good training. Then there were times to play, but I was afraid to enter in, because I was such a sissy.

One morning Pop Patterson told my brother and me, "You boys are going to the sanatorium to visit your mother." What elation we felt! It had been such a long time since we'd seen her. After a long drive, we were told at the sanatorium, "Sorry, boys, we can't let you go up to your mother's room; you have to be sixteen. Tuberculosis is highly infectious. You can stand beneath her window so she'll see you...."

We were not allowed to feel our mother's arms. Only to wave, and call up to her, and see her gazing down at us from her third-floor window. But her smile was full of love. And it was the most love I'd felt in a long while.

The years went by. I grew older and stronger, and I was not picked on as much. But I'll never forget the day when a gang of boys dragged me to the potato fields and demanded, "Okay, Plow, we want a bushel of potatoes, so start digging...and dig 'em with yer *teeth!*"

I struggled to get away, but they tied my hands behind me and held me down, pressing my face in the dirt. There I was, surrounded but alone, humiliated and called all sorts of rotten names, digging up potatoes with my huge buck teeth.

In the years that followed, we saw Mother only occasionally. The wonderful mother whom I dearly loved was slowly, tragically, becoming a stranger to me.

But her letters kept coming regularly, except when she had more surgery. Then we wouldn't hear from her for a month or so. Finally a letter would come: "My dear boys, my thoughts have been so much with you this day....I send all my love. Remember, Jesus loves you, and I am praying for you...."

Sometimes when Mother wrote, it was almost as if she knew what was going on at Glengary. Like the time I decided to smoke on the sly because all the boys did it. You made your own cigarettes from corn silk rolled in toilet paper and lit them in a light socket with steel wool. Soon it became a regular thing with me because it got me in good with the big guys. But then one of Mother's letters arrived, saying, "Your father was such a clean man. You know, he never smoked or drank." So, at the age of twelve, I vowed never to smoke or drink.

"Hey, Keay, wanna go out back for a smoke?" a couple of the guys asked.

"Naw," I said, walking away.

"Hey, why not?" they asked.

"Oh, I dunno, I just don't want to."

As I grew, it became more and more obvious: I was becoming different. Instead of planning ways to run away from Glengary, I slowly began excelling as an athlete. My self-image gradually began to change. I began to do better in school. In fact, I ran for school offices and won. I applied for scholarships and got them. And I didn't beat up on the little kids; they came to me, for protection. I didn't understand it, or even think about it much. But I was different.

It was then time for graduation, time to take advantage of the scholarships I'd won and go to college. But I couldn't. Though I was president of my high school class, I left two months early to take a good job to support Mother, who was going to be released from the sanatorium in six months. It was up to me to make a home for her.

Tuberculosis had claimed many of Mother's ribs, most of both shoulder blades, half of both lungs. But Mother had held on to life, pain-racked and bed-ridden, so she could be with her two boys. After ten long years, we were together again, in Elizabeth, New Jersey, where I took a position with Standard Oil Company.

Morning after morning, as I passed Mother's room, I would see her slowly, painfully, kneeling by her bed. Her thin hands clasped, head bowed in prayer. And I knew that even as Mother's body had weakened over the years, her faith had grown deeper.

One morning, when she heard my step in the hall, she invited me in. Only then did I discover that during all the time we were apart Mother had been closer to me than I could have imagined. "Ike," she said, "God has been good. I see a fine man standing before me, a son to be proud of. God heard my prayers."

Mother told me how, in all the years that she could not be with us, she had prayed for us, constantly. "I asked the

Lord to watch over you boys, to wrap you in His love. Ike, each day I pictured God's shield protecting you."

Then I knew. Mother's prayers had reached across the miles, protecting us, shaping us. A mother I had seldom seen had the greatest influence on my life.

Not long after this, I too met Jesus Christ on my "road to Damascus," as had the Apostle Paul. It was then that some of the missing puzzle pieces started to fit. God had allowed these experiences in my youth to prepare me for a new calling.

So I left Standard Oil and went back to Glengary as a houseparent to boys like myself—to show and tell them about God's love. Three years later I left to enter college to better equip myself for this new calling.

It was during this time that my mother went home to be with her King. God had been gracious and had given us six years together. Immediately following her funeral I learned the startling truth about my father. He had been discovered with a fourteen-year-old girl, an employee; and her father had called the police. They were on the way to arrest him when he took his shotgun and killed himself.

While I was still in college, I met my wife-to-be, Carolyn. After working a number of years in other children's homes, we moved to Bethel Bible Village in Chattanooga, where I was executive director; and we raised four children of our own.

Like the parents of the children at Bethel, my father had committed a crime. I can understand the disappointment and the shame these children feel. I know too how such a child longs for home and for affection. And I know the suffering that a child can endure in an institution. Surely that makes me more sensitive to these children of pain.

We do not have the children long at Bethel. By law they can stay with us approximately eighteen months. However, we do have some leeway, because one or both parents may be in prison for terms longer than that; but eventually each child must leave us.

And as each youngster returns to his home, frequently one of neglect and abuse, sad as I am, I know that I can go on helping and trusting. For I can go to my room and pray. I can ask God to wrap that child in His love, to give him or her the same kind of strong shield that protected my brother and me.

There is a supernatural power that we can draw upon. It flows through us in prayer. It is God's strength, the greatest force in all creation. I know, because I have experienced it.

Cornerstone

The cornerstone of every home,
The most important part,
Is never laid upon the earth,
But in the mother's heart.

LYDIA O. JACKSON

PRAYER THAT FORGIVES

Who, Me?

I need to be forgiven, Lord
So many times a day.
So often do I slip and fall,
Be merciful, I pray!
And help me not be critical
When others' faults I see;
For so many times, my Lord,
The same faults are in me.

AUTHOR UNKNOWN

Break-In!

ANNE FITZPATRICK

It had been an especially pleasant evening, celebrating a birthday with old friends. On the way home, my husband Bill and I happily recalled the surprised expressions when the waitress brought the cake with candles, and everyone around us joined in singing "Happy Birthday." All in all it was such a satisfying evening—until we pulled into our driveway.

As soon as Bill raised the garage door it was obvious something was very wrong. The back door to the garage and a porch door stood wide open. I hurried into the kitchen—another open door—and flipped on the light. The door had been broken and split, and the lock chiseled out.

In the living room, papers were strewn all over, and a bookcase door hung askew, pulled off its hinges. Contents of bedroom drawers spilled out into the hallway. Mute testimony to our burglary lay in the discarded metal lockbox we used for daily expense money, bent and misshapen and, of course, empty.

"Oh, no!" I cried. "I don't believe this." As if by denying I could wipe out the unmistakable evidence before us. Things like this happened to other people, strangers in newspaper accounts, not to us!

"Call the police!" Bill said, hurrying past me and going through all the rooms and closets, then the basement, making sure there was no one still in the house. A foolish move, we were told later by the police, but neither of us was thinking very clearly then.

When Bill came back, we surveyed the damage in each room, being careful, as the police had instructed, not to touch anything. My heart beat faster with each discovery of damage and loss, fury and anger locking horns inside me. In our bedroom, personal belongings tumbled over each other on the floor, on the bed; drawers had been pulled out and emptied. My jewelry box had been left on the bed, open; tangled beads, pins and earrings spilled out, left behind, while my few special pieces had been taken.

"The gold heart you gave me for Christmas!" I wailed. "And my little silver cross, the ring from Italy!" I was close to tears, the taste of anger at this violation of our home was bitter in my throat. Bill, speechless, gently squeezed my shoulder.

The police officer arrived and we went through the house again, stepping over and around piles of clothing, papers, books, as he methodically made out a report.

In the bathroom, medicine cabinet contents had been dumped in the sink; it was impossible to tell what pills were missing. We didn't attempt to enter our grown son's room, where piles of his clothes and belongings blocked the door-way—a wild change from Mike's usual order, with never a thing out of place.

Our teenage son's room, never neat, was now a disaster as T-shirts, jeans, books and records formed mountains on the floor and bed. When he came home, incredulous, he declared his losses: several chains and pendants, an engraved silver medal, precious because it was a gift from his girl friend—and nearly fifty dollars, the Prom money he'd been stashing away under his sweaters.

"At least they didn't take my stereo or my guitar," he said philosophically.

"But now they know where they are," Bill said grimly.

His words alarmed me. "You think they'll come back?"

He shrugged. "I hope not."

There was not much sleep that night. Bill braced the broken doors as securely as possible and we made a start at picking up the mess. *The sooner we restore order,* I thought, *the sooner we can begin to put this invasion out of our minds.*

But it was not that easy. I awoke the next morning after dozing uneasily in the last wee hours, feeling bleary-eyed and exhausted—and deeply depressed. I tried to explain it to Bill. "It's not only losing things, and the money—that's bad enough. But I don't feel safe anymore. What kind of people do things like this?"

He shook his head, no more able than I to understand. "But I know what you mean. The biggest thing they've stolen is our sense of security."

Outside the day was bright and sunny. The neighborhood was normal and peaceful as always, contrasting sharply with the chaos we left inside our home as we went to church.

Throughout the service I searched for words of comfort, something to lighten the gloom I felt. There was nothing. I tried to pray, knowing I should begin to let go my anger and forgive. Experimentally I formed the words, but there was no meaning or truth in them.

Back home we talked to shocked neighbors, who shared our sense of outrage. Break-ins were not unheard of in our town, but this was the first on our street and everyone was concerned. The rest of our day was spent completing the cleanup. Mike's room was once again neat and orderly; the only thing missing was a pillowcase. "They probably meant to fill it with cameras, radios, things like that," Bill figured, again raising the question of a recurrence, and another frightening thought: Perhaps we had interrupted them when we came home!

In the days and weeks that followed, Bill worked on repairs, replacing one door entirely and installing new locks. A sense of normalcy returned—except for the creeping fear that had become part of my life. Every time we went out, I compulsively checked and rechecked our new automatic light-timers, making sure the house would look occupied when darkness came. Turning on outside lights. Locking doors, trying them twice.

In the neighborhood, I watched for strangers, looking with suspicion at anyone I didn't recognize. At bridge club, choir practice, in the supermarket, I couldn't stop talking about it; I found many whose homes had been entered, acquaintances who shared my sense of violation. My anger remained at the sizzling point when I heard things like, "We got new locks, and they came in a cellar window." Or, "We thought it would be a good idea to have floodlights in our yard, and all it did was light the way for them." The bitter tones I heard matched my feelings perfectly.

They. Them. The enemy. Unseen, unheard, *they* had invaded our community, always a few steps ahead of us, ahead of the police. Was there no way to be safe from *them,* the unknown *they* who had become such an unwelcome part of our lives?

Our son Bill was the first to tire of the almost nightly dinner-table topic as I shared these conversations. One night he suggested we pray for the intruders, along with our blessing before the meal.

The idea startled me. "Pray for *them?* How can you say that, after they took the money you worked so hard for!"

He didn't miss a beat in the methodical loading of his plate as he explained: "We should stop dwelling on what happened to *us.* We lost only *things,* but *they've* lost a lot more. They're out of the grace of God by breaking His Law."

I looked at him with surprise, this towering young man who often caught me unaware with his unexpected bursts of wisdom. Then, though I sensed the truth of his words and gave lip service to his prayer, I still could not let go the anger and resentment that simmered like an ugly stew within me.

One day a friend came to visit, a remarkable lady of over seventy. Gladys was youthful, active and energetic, and she had a deep, shining faith I admired. Her home had been broken into too, so she understood my feelings when we talked about our experience. But this conversation was different from all the others I'd had recently. Gladys seemed somehow untouched in the way other people had been—and as I myself was. I sensed no bitterness or hate in her.

She smiled when I told her this. "That's not what God wants in me. God wants me to forgive—and to keep my trust in Him."

Her words, like my son's, rang with a truth I slowly absorbed as I prayed, for I did continue to pray, until the words that began as cotton on my tongue became real. One day, praying our Lord's own words, it struck me how often I repeated phrases unthinkingly, not really paying heed to their meaning. Now, *forgive us our trespasses, as we forgive those who trespass against us* had a specific meaning for *me*. I didn't have to wonder what to do, for He had already instructed me.

By not giving up when prayer was difficult, and by listening to the prayers of others—a seventeen-year-old boy and a seventy-year-old woman—I found that now I *could* pray: *Father, forgive them, and take away my resentment against them*—and know there was real meaning in my prayer.

We still lock our doors and turn lights on when we go out, but our trust is not totally in these things. Our trust is in the Lord and in His Word.

In Psalm 37, I discovered another prayer that speaks to me: "Be not vexed over evildoers.... Trust in the Lord and do good, that you may dwell in the land and enjoy security" (vss. 1, 3, NASB).

The security of being in God's grace.

Strength Twice Over

BRUCE L. JOHNSON

I have fought two incredible battles in my life. Though they were against entirely different adversaries and happened eleven years apart, they were, in a strange way, related.

My first battle was with a man-eating shark. The second was against a deadlier enemy.

The first began on a sunny day in the Bahamas in 1965. I was there on a brief business trip and had decided to take a few hours to catch a little sun on the beach. At the time I was earning my living teaching snorkeling, judo and body building. I had been doing this since World War II when, as heavyweight wrestling champ of the Navy's Third Fleet, I taught combat Rangers survival techniques. Now at the age of thirty-nine, I was in tiptop physical condition—and proud of it.

That afternoon I relaxed on the warm white-sand beach, eyes closed, listening to the sounds of four native children laughing and splashing in the sea. Suddenly, a long harrowing shriek shot me bolt upright. A little girl was thrashing in the water. For only a second I saw her, her red bathing suit in shreds. Then she disappeared. I leaped to my feet and raced toward the surf. A dark dorsal fin knifed toward the other three children.

"Shark! Shark!" I screamed. I spotted a large, pink conch shell in the sand and scooped it up with my left hand as I plunged into the water. I knew that sometimes a shark can be turned away by hitting it on the snout with a club—pounding your hand against its steel-file hide only draws your blood.

I tried to run waist deep in the water, to attract the shark's attention. I grunted with the effort and surged on, but as the shark slid by me toward the children, I made a desperate lunge and the conch shell struck near the shark's tail.

Infuriated, it whirled. For a split second its jaws grabbed at my right arm, but I turned, pulling my arm free. The shark rolled, raking its tough hide across my face, tearing open my lips. I tasted salty blood. Now the shark grabbed at my right arm again just as I drove the conch shell's point deep into its eye, the one vulnerable spot. Startled, the shark released me and I stumbled for shore.

But not fast enough. Suddenly I felt a pull on my right calf. The shark had me. I hopped frantically on my left leg, as the shark dragged me out to sea. I was not aware of the pain as much as the overwhelming viselike pressure of those jaws. My foot slipped from under me and in that last instant of staring wildly into the sky I gulped as much air as I could; then my head went under.

The shark dragged me down, my back and head scraping and bouncing on the sandy bottom. Here, twenty feet down in the crystal water, I could see sand clouds swirling around with each flip of the shark's powerful tail. My eardrums rang with pain, my chest tightened. Once more I tried to slam the shell against the shark's side. This only made it shake the massive head clamped on my leg. Fiery pain went through me.

If I could just get my leg free, I thought. I tried a half sit-up. I grasped the shark's fin with my right hand. Now I was twisted in a seated fetal position. My upright body increased water resistance, slowing us down until the beast stopped. But now I was close again to the shark's jaws. I grasped the shark's snout with one hand and thrust the shell against its lower teeth, trying to pry its mouth open. But nothing happened.

My vision wavered. I knew I couldn't hold my breath much longer. I had only seconds of consciousness left. I couldn't gouge the shark's eyes, for, enraged, it would bite my head or midsection, killing me instantly. Blackness closed in, and I cried out within, *O, God, help me!*

I felt calm. Was this how one felt just before dying?

With a final thrust I dug the conch shell deep into the shark's jaws and wrenched with all my might. They gave a bit! Adrenalin shot through me. I twisted the shell back and forth. Slowly the jaws relaxed. Now! The mouth was open enough to pull out my leg. But at my awkward sitting angle I could not do it without letting go of those jaws.

My impulse was to let them snap, hoping they would chop my foot off and release me. But then, suddenly, miraculously, my leg was free.

Clawing wildly toward the surface, my lungs screaming, I broke into fresh, sweet heavenly air. And that's all I remember. People found me on the beach still " swimming" in the sand. Jabbering excitedly, they told me that I had been underwater for over five minutes.

It took a year for my oozing wounds to heal and before I stopped limping on a severely wrenched knee. All the while I continued to work out with my special exercise program and eventually got my body into athletic shape. Then in December 1976 the second battle began.

I had a stiff neck that bothered me a lot so I went to see a chiropractor, who turned out to be incredibly inept. He had me on a table while he manipulated my neck with his hands.

"That help?" he asked.

"Doesn't seem to," I answered.

"Well, try to relax completely," he said, "and I'll..." At that, he suddenly twisted my neck vigorously. The pain that blazed through me was so great that the ceiling light spun crazily. I was nauseous as he helped me down from the table.

"You'll be okay in no time," he assured me, handing me some vitamin tablets he said would ease my condition.

I drove home using only my right arm since my left had lost its coordination.

When my wife Shari, who is a nurse, saw me stagger in our front door, she thought I'd had a stroke. She called an ambulance. At the hospital I groaned in constant pain while I underwent tests. Finally, conferring neurosurgeons determined that the manipulation of my neck had occluded the vertebral artery causing loss of oxygen to the brain. "A brain stem infarction," they said.

I had gone from a healthy, physically strong person to what seemed an invalid in a quick snap of a neck. I'd lost my sense of balance and coordination on my left side. My heart rate, blood pressure and bladder function were affected, and I suffered from choking spells. I had no feeling on my right side when pricked with pins. When standing, the room seemed to spin and I was nauseous.

After two hospitalizations totaling about six weeks, interspersed with painful tests, I had much time to think about the man who had put me in this condition. When I remembered how he nonchalantly handed me those vitamin tablets, anger swelled within me. I had a burning hatred for him, which was unlike me, as I never before carried grudges.

Then I would recall my neurosurgeons' verdict. "If you don't get better in a few months, well..." and my anger festered. The "few months" went by, but instead of improving I discovered that now I had double vision. "A delayed result of the brain stem infarction and not unusual," said my doctors. None of them would predict just what permanent brain damage had been done. Only time would tell, but it did not look good.

More weeks dragged by, then months. Depression set in as I tried to cope with my limitations, wearing a black patch over one eye to improve the double vision and a cervical collar to lessen the severe headaches. I had to use a cane because of my loss of balance.

I diligently followed special therapy exercises I had devised, since teaching exercises was my profession. However, my progress was painfully slow.

I avoided mirrors. The sight of the pale, drawn figure with the black eyepatch and neck collar sickened me. And my anger against the man responsible for it never left me.

One day when my vision began to improve, Shari brought me a Bible. She had been patiently waiting until I could read again. She was a deep-believing Christian who had always tried, gently, to make me understand her love for God. But I had never really tried to understand. I was the black belt judo champion, the man who had fought a ten-foot shark—and won. Somehow I'd even forgotten how I cried out to God during that battle. I believed in physical strength, not spiritual.

Now, however, I began to read her Bible and for the first time in my life, God's Word really began to mean something to me.

Soon I began to accompany Shari to a good "Bible believing and preaching" church. At first I found the services a soothing diversion; it was good to be out again and be with friendly people. But as I continued reading the

Bible more, I looked forward to church more, until, one day in early April 1978, I walked down our church aisle and accepted Jesus Christ as my Lord and Savior.

By now over a year had passed since my "accident." I was still struggling with exercises, suffering constant headaches and vertigo. My left arm had hardly improved and both legs were still extremely weak. I stayed in bed or in a chair much of the time, still carrying hate for the man who had done this to me. On the night of May 19, 1978, I was lying in bed listening to the radio. Shari had had a very busy day because of a private duty case and was fast asleep beside me. It was a little after ten o'clock and I was listening to *The 700 Club*. The program's host, Pat Robertson, and his guest, Demos Shakarian, head of the Full Gospel Business Men's Fellowship were reading people's prayer requests.

"Here's one from a man in Oregon," said Robertson, who read a letter in which the writer described having the same neck injury as mine.

I felt sorry for this man, and when Robertson said, "Let's pray for this man right now," I forgot about my own condition and lifted up my hands and began praying for the man.

As I did I thought of the Scripture that our pastor had repeated so often: "And when ye stand praying, forgive, if ye have aught against any" (Mark 11:25). It struck me that here I was praying for God's help when I hadn't forgiven the man who had hurt me.

And so, my hands still raised, I relinquished the hatred. "O Father," I said, "I forgive him because I know You have forgiven him and You have forgiven my sins, too." As I lay there, hot tears on my cheeks, a startling thing happened. My hands, still above my head, suddenly felt as if they'd touched a bare electric wire. It seemed as if a jolt of lightning shot through me. An excruciating pain seared my neck, so intense that, gritting my teeth, I started to get up to get a pain pill. Wincing, I put my feet on the floor and automatically reached for my cane.

Then, as I stood up, I got another shock. The pain was gone! I had no more dizziness! My vertigo had disappeared. For the first time in a year and a half the room was not spinning. I stood transfixed. I wasn't dreaming, for the radio crackled on; the lamp glowed on the bedside table, Shari still peacefully slept.

My legs! They felt strong again. I gingerly walked across the room, testing them. I didn't limp! I stood on one foot and then on the other. I didn't fall!

God...could He have...?

Trembling, I had to find out if this was real. I rummaged in the closet, found my jogging shoes, laced them on. Then I slipped out of the house onto our street.

At first I walked cautiously, then gradually quickened my pace. I wasn't even stumbling! Then with renewed confidence I ran. That verse in Isaiah flowed through my mind: "But they that wait upon the Lord shall renew their strength; they shall mount up with wings as eagles; they shall run, and not be weary; and they shall walk, and not faint" (Isaiah 40:31). In long easy strides I loped down the empty street, the cool night air rushing against my face, my legs and body moving rhythmically, painlessly, freely.

After half a mile, I returned to the house, leaping and exulting, eager to share this healing. I woke Shari and her eyes widened; then she, too, was crying in joy. Together we knelt at the bedside and thanked God for His healing.

And so, those were the two monsters I'd fought. I'd battled a shark for my physical life; I'd battled the monster of hate for my soul.

My Father, the Fisherman

PATRICIA ZIMMERMAN

There it was again. As I slowed to a stop at the light on Route 7, in Connecticut, the joy of the day vanished. The same dark feeling slipped over me. It was never far away. "O God," I cried aloud, "You've given me a new life. I have a job, my children, a loving fellowship. Why does this sadness keep coming back?"

The light turned green and as the car in front of me pulled forward, I glanced at its license plate. The number was 309, the street address of my childhood home in Teaneck, New Jersey: 309 Warwick Avenue. The memories rushed in.

A Dutch colonial house. My gentle mother, my older brother Ed, and ... my father ...

I heard again my father's booming laugh when he'd come home from his work as a car salesman, his powerful arms lifting me high, his bright gray eyes sparkling. "Here's my Little One!" he'd say. I loved my father then. When I'd bring home a drawing from school, I'd wait breathlessly for his response. His approval was my heaven, his smile a crowning victory. He was a commanding, talented man, champion skeet shooter and chess player, a fine photographer and an ardent fisherman. How he loved fishing!

But then, at sixteen, my parents' marriage split apart. My father left us, and the light of my world went with him. My mother worked through the days and wept through the nights. For me 309 Warwick became a prison of grief. I longed to break free.

Soon Ed left for college and I fled to New York City for the good life, to drink in the glamour of new friends, new parties, new freedom and the swift magic of alcohol. Soon I had everything, a fine husband, children, a home. But it wasn't enough. I continued to drink. The swift magic turned to slow poison, and the freedom I sought in alcohol became a prison with no reprieve. My marriage failed, my world split apart.

Then a God-given fellowship of compassionate people who understood my problem with alcohol led me out of that prison. They taught me to pray for the faith I had lost, and I found it in Jesus, the Christ ...

The car with the 309 license plate turned off and vanished in the darkness.

Now my mother was gone. Both she and my brother had been dead for years and I'd long ago lost touch with my father.

Your father, came the words, unspoken; but words I seemed to hear. *Heal your relationship with your father,* came the command.

"I can't!" I said, speaking out loud. "I haven't seen him for years, I don't know where he is. He's probably dead by now." I gripped the steering wheel. "And I don't want to see him again, ever."

How many times had I thought about my father. Reading the Bible I'd think of him and get angry. I'd remember the passage in Matthew, where Jesus speaks about fathers and their children. "Or what man of you, if his son asks him...for a fish, will give him a serpent?" (7:9, 10 RSV). Well Dad had given me a serpent. "Explain *that* one to me, Lord!"

I remembered the commandment, "Honor your father," and my heart was cold.

Again it came, an insistent order: *You must heal your relationship with your father.*

At my fellowship meeting the time came to reveal my dilemma. "I haven't seen my father in seventeen years," I said. "What could we say to each other after all this time?"

"How old would he be if he is still alive?" a friend asked.

"Oh, in his late seventies."

"Well, then," she said gently, "you might not have much time left."

I recoiled at her answer, but I knew what I had to do.

I phoned a cousin in Albany. After the usual small talk, I finally got around to it. "Do you know anything about my father?" I asked, my throat tightening.

"Well, we know he's living on Long Island with his sister," she said, then added, "Funny thing, Pat; his cousin Vera said he had been asking about you."

With trembling hands I dialed my father's cousin. We hadn't talked in years. She was happy to hear from me but said sadly that my father was in a nursing home on Long Island.

"He's had a second stroke," she said, "and has lost his speech and desire to eat. I'm afraid it's just a matter of time."

When I mentioned going to see him, she said, "Oh, I don't think he'd know you, Patty; he's too far gone."

"Well," I said, "at least I'd like to call the nursing home."

She gave me the number and the nurse who answered confirmed that it was "just a matter of days."

Suddenly, I felt an urgency to see my father, this man who had once meant so much to me. I had a florist wire him a flowering plant. And then, as soon as I could, I drove from Connecticut to Long Island.

When I pulled up in front of the nursing home I was filled with dread. What do you say to someone you haven't seen for seventeen years ... to someone you've hated for so long?

I walked down the nursing home corridor, my heart pounding as I approached his door. When I stepped into his room I was stunned by what I saw.

There was my father, the once tall sportsman with the booming voice, now a small, hunched figure propped up in a chair. Tubes snaked from a body that shook with tremors. My plant sat on the bureau; it, too, was dying.

I sat down next to him and took a thin, cold hand. My voice choked. "Daddy?"

I looked into his vacant eyes. There was no sign of recognition. His mind was lost somewhere.

I held his shaking hand, and as I sat there, I knew the hate I'd borne him all those years was gone. I thought of how my mother had suffered when she died.

"O Lord," I prayed, "please don't let him suffer."

Squeezing his hand, I said: "Daddy, it's going to be okay. I love you. I love you."

I stood and wrote a note to his sister, giving my phone number, and placed it on the bureau. Then I stepped back to his chair and, laying my hands on his thin shoulders, I prayed: "O God, bless him, please bless him."

When I arrived home late that evening, my son told me the nursing home had called to say my father had been rushed to the hospital. He was dying.

I wept that night. I wept for the lost years we could have been friends, for the hate I had bottled up inside me. I wept for families everywhere who never forgive one another.

At a prayer meeting two days later I spoke out to the Lord: "I offer up my father, who is dying."

Something broke within me at that moment. I felt at last the peace I had longed for. Now the hate was completely gone. I was filled with love for my father.

On Sunday, a week later, there was another phone call from the nursing home on Long Island. "Mrs. Zimmerman?"

"Yes." I dreaded what the nurse was about to tell me. And then a voice, loud and clear.

"Patty?" The voice was familiar, so familiar that I found it difficult to believe.

It was my father!

And he had a list of orders for me! In rapid fire he asked for my address, told me to call his sister, call his friends, send his clothes to the nursing home and then he put the nurse back on the phone.

"We haven't the slightest idea of what happened to him," she said in a bewildered tone. " All we know is that he was dying when he went to the hospital and he came back well. Why, he's walking the halls, talking up a storm to everyone. He even has a chess tournament going on in the day room."

I could hardly control myself from laughing. It was so like him.

"Everyone here calls him Lazarus," the nurse giggled.

Within a few weeks my father had left the nursing home and he and his sister moved to Maine where he began a wonderful new life in an area he had always loved. When I drove up to see him, he told me he had no memory of my visit to the nursing home. "But that was the turning point, Patty," he said. He looked wonderful!

That was the beginning of our new relationship. We never talked about the past; there was no need. It was over. Somehow I knew his feelings, his suffering, his regrets. And I knew he understood mine. God had given us both new lives.

One thing was clear: he was healed not only in body, but in spirit. One year when he was having trouble with shingles, I told him our church group would pray for him. "Thanks, Patty," he chuckled, "I'll know if it's working."

His letters had a robust humor, full of political opinions and stuffed with photographs he took on his many trips across New England. Knowing my love of poetry, he proudly sent me a photo he'd taken of the home of Edwin Arlington Robinson in Gardiner, Maine. And I sent him a book on fishing, as he still was an inveterate fisherman and Maine was proving a paradise.

But I was not prepared for the biggest surprise.

It came in a bulky letter from Dad. In his strong handwriting he excitedly described his eightieth birthday on which he enjoyed "my greatest fishing trip ever ...

"We caught a lot, Patty," he wrote, "but your old dad was honored with the prize catch of the day, a forty-inch salmon! I've got to believe, Patty," he continued, "that Somebody up there must like me a little bit." A thrill ran through me.

And then, as I unfolded more of the letter, a photograph fell out and I picked it up. It was "the catch of the day."

There in my hand was the glistening salmon in living color.

"Thank You," I whispered. "Just as You promised. He's given me my fish, just as You promised!"

Change of Heart

Wronged and wounded by a friend,
I cried to You in prayer;
Asked for justice, stretched my hand
To You. Yours wasn't there.

Wronged and wounded by a friend,
I sought to understand;
Prayed that I might love, forgive.
You reached and took my hand.

HELEN A. STRICKLAND

Prayer That's Honest

O God of earth and altar,
Bow down and hear our cry;
Our earthly rulers falter,
Our people drift and die;
The walls of gold entomb us,
The swords of scorn divide,
Take not thy thunder from us,
But take away our pride.

G. K. CHESTERTON (1874–1936)

The Truth Session

IDELLA BODIE

Swallowing hard, I stood at my dormitory window and watched the wind push snow-swirls down the small mountain and over the main campus of Mars Hill Junior College. My deep sighs—so much a part of my life for the past months—made frosty patches on the glass.

A year ago I'd chosen this college north of Asheville, North Carolina, from catalogs in the high school library. The pictures of majestic mountains reaching into hazy skies, the rock walls, and tree-lined, winding roads had appealed to my quiet nature. A shy girl of sixteen and a lover of books, I dreamed of being an English teacher.

Now I ached with homesickness that covered me like the snow I saw closing over the mountain laurel. I'd expected to miss my South Carolina birthplace and my family, but not to be overwhelmed as I was now. Homesickness— real homesickness—is an affliction that can cause deep psychic pain. I was truly suffering.

Several times each week I wrote my mother, pouring out my heartache, struggling not to ask to break our agree-

ment that I would wait until Christmas for my first visit
home. Sending me to college was a hardship for my family,
and I knew the long bus trip would impose an unnecessary
expense. I also knew that if I went home now I would not
come back.

Growing up on a farm, the youngest child, had made
me an introspective person. I had spent all of my hours
away from school in the pasture with its sweet smell of
grass, tunnels made by bullace vines, and violets tucked
beside cooling streams. I stroked calves and watched
piglets root for dinner, wandered in the haylofts and corn-
cribs, and rode horseback. Now I was over two hundred
miles from that dear, familiar place, in the midst of
strangers. I cried myself to sleep every night.

It was in this dejected state that I turned from the window and trudged off to the bedtime devotions held on each
floor of the dorm by a member of the Baptist Student
Union. Most of the girls gathered in the room were already
dressed in nightgowns or pajamas with their hair in curlers.
After Scripture reading and prayers, the group began the
usual chitchat, ranging from "secret passions" (boys who
were admired and didn't know it) to Christmas vacation
plans. I perched on the sidelines thinking, *Oh, if only I can
last that long.*

About that time a tall blonde named Sally, whom I recognized as a music major from down the hall, spoke up suddenly. "Say, why don't we have a *truth session?*"

"A what?" several girls asked at one time. Even I found
my curiosity piqued.

"We used to do it all the time at slumber parties back home," Sally went on. "Really. A lot of good can come from it if everybody takes it the right way."

Despite some groans, everyone seemed intrigued.

Before we knew it, Sally had us seated in a circle. The idea, she explained, was to go around the circle telling the truth about each person.

"Okay now," she said, "everybody has to agree beforehand not to get upset but to accept what is said in good faith and work on the problem. Just remember," she added, "the truth is meant to be *helpful*."

Sally started things rolling by saying she already knew that her habit of humming constantly irritated others—and since she had begun to work on that, she preferred the challenge of a different problem.

Then her roommate obliged by telling Sally she talked too much—and that in her estimation humming was better than nonstop chatter.

The tone of friendly banter caught on as the truth-telling went around the circle. The next girl needed to keep her room tidier, another to be more punctual. And, tactfully, each negative comment was prefaced by a compliment.

I felt a flush rising as all eyes focused on me. How had I let myself get into this situation? Wasn't I feeling bad enough already?

"Idella is a beautiful girl..." the speaker hesitated. I recognized her as a girl in my psychology class. "But she's selfish."

A fainting feeling began passing down my body in warm waves. *How could she say such a thing? Why, she didn't even know me.*

"You mean *stuck-up,*" somebody else said.

My mind whirred. Numbness spread over me.

"You just think that because she's so reserved," Sally offered good-humoredly. "She's shy, can't you see?"

I don't remember anything else about the episode except Sally's admonition that no one must ever, ever refer to what went on this night. Only the receiver was to remember.

Back in my room, I flung myself on my bed and lay there staring at the ceiling. How could they say such things? I had never done anything to them. In fact, I had hardly spoken to any of them. *Selfish,* the girl had said, and no one had denied it. Instead, they had made things even worse by saying I was "stuck-up."

All that night I alternately cried and tried to think rationally. Near daybreak I knew what I would do. The circle of truth had made the decision for me. I would leave this school immediately.

Skipping breakfast, I bundled up and headed down toward the registration office. I wanted to be there when it opened to tell the dean of women about my decision.

By the time I reached the administration building I was shivering from the bitter cold. I had been too eager; the offices were not open yet. I hugged my body against the biting wind; I tried pressing myself against a recessed door adjacent to the offices. Then I thought of the little chapel on the other side of the street. It would not be locked and it would be a place out of the cold until the office opened.

In the warmth of the chapel, I looked about. The one narrow window facing east threw a long bar of light across a table with an opened Bible that stood in the center of the room.

Something about the stillness and the serenity of the soft light affected me. Before I knew it, I was on my knees telling God about my resentments and self-pity. "I've tried, Lord," I said. "You know I've tried."

An echo of the words from the night before rang in my ears. *Selfish. Stuck-up.* Was I really like that? I was sure I wasn't. But if I wasn't like that, then what was I really like?

I looked at the open Bible before me, and suddenly the words of Jesus came into my mind: "Ye shall know the truth, and the truth shall make you free" (John 8:32).

The truth shall make you free? What *was* the truth about me? How did I appear to others?

And suddenly I saw it clearly. In truth, I had spent so much time thinking only of myself and my homesickness that I had built a wall around myself that kept friendship out. I had pictured myself as a quiet, shy person who wrote her thoughts in journals, while others saw me as a person too self-centered to share feelings or to offer understanding.

Now, through the candid words of a classmate, the Lord had allowed me a glimpse of this fixation on myself.

As I knelt before the Bible, I felt my loneliness begin to drain away. God had been with me all along. He was waiting for me to make room in my heart for His love, a love that would warm others.

When I came out of the chapel, slivers of sunshine were bouncing off the snow in sparkling light shards. I was already running back up toward my dorm when I realized I'd forgotten all about going by the registration office.

Back in my room, I wrote to my mother. For the first time since leaving home, I did not burden her with my homesickness. I said, "I want you to know how much I appreciate the sacrifices you are making for me to go to college." I spoke of the snow flurries the day before and of my studies.

On the way to my first class, I knocked timidly at the door of my neighbor's room. She yelled, "Come in!" and I stuck my head in to ask if she'd like to study for the psychology test with me.

"You bet," she said with a surprised grin.

Changing was not easy for an insecure sixteen-year-old. But I began to make a conscious effort to get to know the other girls on the hall. When I felt the urge to draw within my shell and remain quiet, I would ask someone a question about herself. Gradually I learned that in sharing with others I pushed away my problem of homesickness.

And every night I breathed a special prayer for knowing the deepest truth of all: that Jesus loves me, and I have a commitment to share that love with others.

How could I be a teacher, like Him, without being willing to give of myself?

How to Do What You Really Want to Do

VIRGINIA LIVELY

I looked at the figures on the bathroom scale in dismay. I had to admit that despite my best intentions, I was continuing to gain weight. I trudged into the living room, pushed some magazines off the couch and sank down in despair. "O Lord," I sighed, "I have tried and tried to lose weight, but I just can't do it on my own. You'll have to help me."

An odd thing happened when I asked for His help. *Virginia,* He seemed to say to me as I prayed, *you just want to overeat more than you want to lose weight.*

I was startled and defensive, but I had to admit it was true. I often invented reasons for eating. An upsetting phone call, anxiety about a speech I was to give, *anything* seemed to be a good excuse for sending me off to the refrigerator. And eating itself often got out of hand. Instead of stopping at two cookies, I'd eat the whole bag. Now I had to confess that it wasn't just a matter of will power. It was a question of which did I want more: to eat or lose weight?

So I started to say a different prayer: "O Lord, from this moment on help me to truly *want* to lose weight."

It took time, but gradually I found I wasn't thinking about food as much anymore. If ever I'd reach for that refrigerator door handle between meals, I seemed to hear Him saying: *Which do you want more, Virginia, food or a slimmer body?*

Little by little, as I began to lose weight, I started applying that crucial question to other areas of my life. Exercise, for instance. Again, in my prayers to God, He let me see that I'd rather sit and lounge than exercise. And again I confessed that this was so, asking Him to change my desire.

Sure enough, one morning as I stood at my kitchen window, I felt a yearning to go outside. I put my jacket on and walked around the block. I enjoyed it so much that I did it again the next day. The next week, I increased my daily walk to two blocks, then four. On my walks, I liked the feel of the sun and the breeze and the sight of the pretty flower gardens in my neighborhood. I felt alive.

Then I began to notice how cluttered my house was. I had complained about it to myself for years, making some very good excuses. I couldn't get to it because of speaking engagements. I was too busy.

Can you guess what I started to hear from the Lord? *No, Virginia, you don't get to it because you don't want to. You want it just as it is.*

"My word!" I said to myself. "No, I *don't* want a messy house." Again I prayed, "Lord, I know it's Your will that this house be in order. Please help me."

I began to clean house and enjoy it. I started first with the little bedroom I call my office. Then in the storage room I threw out the old paint cans I'd been saving. I even began coming across people I could give things to, things they needed and could use.

And so I've found three essential steps in breaking irksome habits:

1. *Confess* that you've been doing what you've *wanted* to do, not what you thought you should be doing.

2. *Decide* what you really want.

3. *Pray.* Ask the Lord to help you with your true desire. He will enhance that desire, just as He did for me that morning when I looked out the window and felt the longing to go out and take a walk.

The other day, my daughter telephoned me, complaining, "Mother, my house is a mess. I don't know if I'll ever get it straight. These children won't pick up anything, I can't get the laundry done and—"

I stopped her. "Honey, let me tell you about the "I-wants'..."

The Fallen Bird's Nest

SUE MONK KIDD

It was scarcely midafternoon, yet the doctor's waiting room was dark. Outside, enormous black clouds roiled and rolled. A storm was on the way. From my green chair in the corner, I felt strangely part of it—the peculiar darkness, the impending storm, clouds rumbling like a rockslide. In more ways than one, it seemed things were about to topple.

I'd come here because of a lump in my breast. I'd discovered it myself and naturally I'd gone to the family doctor hoping he would pat my hand and say, " Nothing to it." Instead, he'd sent me here, to a surgeon.

Lump. I turned the word over in my mind. It always rang the same ominous note...striking a particular chord buried years before when I'd worked as a nurse. It was a memory I never tampered with. Now it was all coming back with the swiftness of a dream.

But Mrs. Holly was no dream. She was literally the first patient I ever had. She'd had a lump, one that began her long battle with cancer. I cared for her for months. In all that time she never had a visitor. One morning as I brought her breakfast tray, I found her leaning at the window. Against the breaking light her frail little silhouette reminded me of the dark contours of pain and longing that seemed to shape so much of her life.

"Where is God?" she asked, gazing far into the distance as if she might catch His presence vanishing over the horizon.

"Why, He's right here with us," I replied, serving up the answer almost as easily as her meal.

She turned and looked at me intently. "I wonder..." she whispered. And at that moment I felt nearly as lost and unconvinced as she did. We never spoke of it again, but the episode always hung unfinished between us, like a puzzle you can't solve or a book you never complete.

I sat by her bed as she died. There were just the two of us. I kept thinking about the question she'd asked that day. Maybe it was my imagination, but I felt as if she was thinking of it too. She was too weak to talk, but near the end she gave me the faintest little smile. Then she closed her eyes and died. All alone, it seemed.

I felt unsettled for weeks afterward. Sometimes my eyes mysteriously filled with tears when I passed her room. "I know she was your first patient," a colleague said. "But you can't get emotionally involved like this." I took her advice. I packed up the hurt and unanswered questions and buried them. All that remained of the experience was a queer little dread that twisted in the pit of my stomach at every mention of the word *lump*....

The nurse's words cut through my thoughts. "Mrs. Kidd, the doctor will see you." I marched after her, trying to shake the old, disquieting memory.

After the exam the surgeon cleared his throat. "We need to take out the lump and get a biopsy," he said.

"Do you think it could be ... malignant?" I asked.

He smiled gently. "Now, Sue, most lumps turn out to be benign, and I think it's entirely probable yours will be also. But you know I can't make absolute promises."

Surgery was set. I would check into the hospital in a few days.

An odd stillness squeezed the air as I scuffed my shoes across the parking lot. There wasn't a breath of wind. I told myself I had every reason to be hopeful, that Mrs. Holly was just one person, that thousands go through this and come out fine. I told myself all the reasonable things. But it was not a reasonable moment. Alone in the car, the little dread turned into a fear that overwhelmed all the logic in the world.

As I pulled into the driveway at home, the first drops broke from the swollen skies. I spotted my son in the backyard pulling his bicycle out of the rain. "Hurry, it's already coming down!" I yelled.

Bob bumped his wheels over the roots of the oak tree, scaring up a chipmunk that lived in the woodpile. "Will the storm hurt the chipmunks?" he called.

"They'll be okay."

"How about *them?*" He was gazing into the crook of an oak limb, at a bird's nest he'd discovered the week before.

Dear God, life was collapsing on my head and my son was standing in the rain worrying about birds and chipmunks. "Yes, the entire animal kingdom will be fine!" I practically shouted. "Now come on!"

The incongruity continued on all evening—small inconsequential details going right on as though no threat existed.

Finally, with everyone asleep, I tossed on my pillow, listening to the rain crash on the roof. Raveled in my thoughts and fears were old haunting images of Mrs. Holly and traces of the unsettled feeling I'd had after she died. That unfinished business...it made no sense.

Not wanting to wake my husband, I wandered to the den, where I sank into a chair. Lightning irradiated the panes with light, illuminating the backyard. For an instant I glimpsed the oak pitching and swaying in the night. *Nothing is really certain in this world,* I thought. I drew my knees beneath my chin as the wind whirred and slapped like helicopter blades in the blackness. And suddenly Mrs. Holly's question blew out of the storm. "Where is God?" Only this time it was no longer an echo lost in the years between us. It was my very own question.

"Where are You?" I cried, startled to hear the words coming from my lips. Even more startled to realize how abandoned I'd felt since discovering the lump. It wasn't just facing life's uncertainties that seemed so fearful. It was facing them alone, without God.

Now a door was opening inside me and before I could stop it, the rest spilled out too. The part I'd never been able to put into words. "And where were You back then when Mrs. Holly looked for You?" I whispered. "If You weren't there for *her*, how do I know You'll be here for *me?*" The awful doubt I'd carried inside for so long trailed off in the shadows.

I felt terrible saying it, almost disloyal. In all my life I'd never blurted out a doubt to God. But there was relief in it too. I went back to bed much lighter, as if a clean new space had been created inside me.

The next morning a bit of sunshine dribbled over a cloud. The children scurried out to play. It wasn't long before I heard shouts erupting from the backyard. "Mama! Come quick!"

I leaped a row of brown puddles. And there beneath the oak, at the tips of the children's tennis shoes, lay the bird's nest. Sprawled beside it were two newborn birds. They groped in the grass, looking helpless and wet. I looked at them in dismay. Just what I needed.

"They fell from the tree!" cried Bob. "And you said they'd be okay. You said—"

"I know," I interrupted, remembering the branches lashing in the wind.

There was nothing else to do. I knelt down, scooped the hatchlings into my hands and placed them in the nest. But as I knelt over that little scene, it came to me. One small fragment of an old familiar verse. "One of them shall not fall on the ground without your Father" (Matthew 10:29). For a moment I didn't move, as I held the words in my mind and felt them descend slowly into my heart—into a clean, new space, which before had been a closet for my doubt. I could hear God answering the doubts and questions deep inside, answering them in the gentlest sort of way. "I'm here...I've been here all along."

I tucked the nest into the ivy that draped the brick fence, while the children agonized over whether their mother would find it. But the next day she appeared on the fence with a beakful of food. The birds were fine.

And I was, too. Just as the doctor predicted, the lump was benign. But just as important, the episode helped me understand something. If God seems far away in the midst of a dark moment, it's not He who's missing, but my ability to perceive Him. And sometimes the way is cleared simply by offering God one's doubts with a gentle honesty.

Somehow I think that's how it happened for Mrs. Holly. For, as that old memory began to heal inside me, I grew sure she'd found the assurance of God's presence. In fact, I wonder if that faint smile she gave me before she died was meant to tell me so.

Yes, I think she knew, just as I do now. No one is alone.

Out of the Sky

STEVE DAVIS

Visibility was less than marginal the afternoon of November 17, 1976. Not one of us sitting around the flight business office at Hunt's Airport in Portland, Texas, would have bet more than a dollar that a plane could get through to land. No one counted on the little Cessna 172 that came barreling out of a sky as dark and choppy as lentil soup. And I couldn't have imagined how it would change my life forever.

I'd awakened that morning feeling pretty pleased with myself. One year before, when I'd arrived from North Carolina, my life savings easily fit into my pocket. But now, at twenty-three, I had it made—or so I thought. I was a flight instructor with my own thriving flight school, and three airplanes of my own. One of my first Texas students had been a beautiful young woman named Linda Peters, who was now my girlfriend. I had more money than I needed. That day I was so self-satisfied that I didn't even mind that it was too cold and rainy to do any flight instructing. "Northers" often hit southern Texas, but they blow on through within a couple of days.

Bad weather for flight instructing is perfect weather for indulging in a little "hangar flying." So I pulled on my bomber jacket and drove over to the Chicken Shack to pick up lunch for the boys—Jess, the retiree who did our books; Ray; and A.A., who in his sixties was finally learning to fly. By the time I got back it was drizzling and so foggy I couldn't even make out Corpus Christi across the bay. Only instrument-rated pilots could fly in this weather, and they'd have to fly into the bigger, tower-controlled Corpus Christi International.

But inside, the atmosphere was convivial. I put out the chicken, and we all sat around on the fraying vinyl furniture and jawed a bit, telling tall tales and patching the world's woes. Jess and Ray went on ribbing A.A. for taking up flying so late in life.

"Well, better late than never," A.A. said. "Not like Steve. To hear him tell it, he could fly before he could walk."

"That's right," I agreed. "My mom and dad said the only time I'd sit still was in an airplane with them." And I told them how I'd spent most of my childhood in Mexico, where my dad had been a missionary pilot. As I talked I could see myself as a ten-year-old in shirtsleeves, riding along dusty roads with my dad to the airstrip outside of Guadalajara. How often I'd pictured turning the corner and rumbling up to the most beautiful sight in the world—our Fairchild 24. A hunk of junk, really, an old tail-dragger my dad bought for $300. He'd hung a radial engine in it—an old round one with lots of horsepower. Nice and noisy.

"Let's load'er up, Steve!" Dad would call, and we'd put in as many crates of supplies as the plane could carry. Then we'd strap in. There wasn't a takeoff that didn't scare—and thrill—me to the bottom of my sandals. Then we'd be up in the open skies, flying over villages and rain forests and mountain ranges. "I think I'll take a few winks, Steve. Hold'er steady," Dad would say, and he'd doze off—or pretend to—while I held course and altitude. Then he'd set her down in some mountaintop village that had been waiting for the supplies we were bringing.

The guys grunted their appreciation of the scene and I quit talking. But there was something there, in my past, that was gnawing at me, and had been for the past few months. As the others went on talking, I mentally stayed behind in that mountaintop village.

After we unloaded the supplies, Dad would gather the natives around, and tell them about *Jesus Cristo, El Salvador.* I soaked up every word. Jesus Christ had been intensely real to me then. I even thought of myself as a missionary, and all I wanted to do was to grow up and be a man like Nate Saint, a pilot I'd read about in a book my parents had given me. The book was *Through Gates of Splendor* by Elisabeth Elliot (New York: Harper & Row, 1961). It was the story of five missionaries, including Mrs. Elliot's husband, who were martyred by Indians in Ecuador in 1956. It was a moving story of faith and adventure, but the part I almost committed to memory was about my hero, Nate

Saint, the young pilot who flew them on their missions. I admired him so much that when I held course for my dad, I'd imagine I *was* Nate Saint, flying much-needed supplies to remote corners of the jungle. Soon, it *would* be me!

Just the memory of that time brought a catch to my throat. I'd been so joyful, so confident of God. I'd had a faith like Nate Saint's, worth risking everything for. But somewhere along the line...what had happened to it? I lived in the adult world now, a world of doubts and conflicts and temptations. Since there was no one around to help me deal with these nagging doubts, I found it much easier to ignore them. So I had quit worrying about Christianity and devoted all my attention to flying. But where my faith once had been, there was now a profound sense of loss. I felt empty inside.

Recently I'd come across my old copy of *Through Gates of Splendor.* I'd tried to put the book away, but I couldn't shake the sadness that gripped me—because of Nate's death, because of my own loss of faith. Finally I stopped and said the first prayer I'd said in years: "Now, wait a minute, God. Something tells me You're not real. I'd really like to know You the way I thought I did. I want to have the faith I used to have. But I just can't blindly accept that stuff I grew up with. If You'll let me know that You're real, I will serve You, but I've got to know. I can't pretend."

I didn't feel any answer to my prayer. In fact, I didn't feel anything at all. And that made me angry.

No, I'd thought, *it's all a farce. My boyhood hero, Nate Saint, wasted his life. He died for nothing.*

The book had fallen open to the photo section, and I'd looked at the picture of Nate's son, Steve, then five years old. *That kid would probably be about my age now,* I'd figured. *And if the truth be known, he's probably in worse shape spiritually today than I am.*

In disgust and anger I'd put the book away. Now, sitting in the flight business office on this stormy day, I was still angry.

I tried to shake those thoughts and get back into the conversation. Wouldn't the guys laugh if they knew I'd been asking for proof from a nonexistent God—and that I was all torn up because no answer was forthcoming?

"Wa-a-ll, we might as well close up," said Jess. "The rain's only getting worse."

As we all stood to start closing, Julio, one of Mr. Hunt's workers, stopped in. He liked to talk with me, because I was one of the few folks around who was fluent in Spanish, his native tongue. "*Hola,* Steve," he said. "*Aqui viene un avion loco.*"

We looked out through the rain, and sure enough, a little Cessna 172 was dropping out of the sky toward the airstrip.

"Nice day for a little scud-running," laughed A.A. But we all breathed a sigh of relief when the plane touched down safely and taxied in.

"Probably drug runners," decided Ray. "What other business would have you out flying on a day like this?"

A few minutes later the pilot and the passenger swung the door open and came in, dripping. They were both young and clean-cut.

"Hello," the pilot started. "We barely made it in. I'm not instrument rated—I didn't think I was going to find an uncontrolled airport. Can we tie down? Is there a motel in town where we can stay and wait for better weather?"

"We're just closing," said Jess. "But yeah, you can tie down." A.A. and Ray were already heading out.

"There's a motel in Portland," I said. "If you hurry up, I'll wait and drive you over." I turned back to Julio to continue our conversation about the weather. "*Este tiempo esta malo.*"

"*Y peligroso, tambien,*" agreed the pilot. "*Yo no débía haber volado el avión con un dia como este* [I had no business flying on a day like this]."

The three of us had talked for a few minutes before I realized how odd it was that the pilot, a blond, blue-eyed Anglo, was speaking fluent Spanish. "Where'd you learn the language?" I asked.

"My parents were missionaries in Ecuador," he said. "I grew up there."

"Really?" I asked. "Did you ever hear of any of those missionaries who were martyred down there twenty years ago?"

"One of them was his dad," the passenger said.

"Oh, yeah?" I pursued. "What's your name?"

"Steve Saint," he said.

The boy from the book!

All the air went out of me, like I'd been punched in the chest. It was as if God had used that book to kindle my faith as a child, and now, when I had deeper questions, the boy in the book flew out of its pages and stood here before me!

But did he have any faith? Or was this a cruel coincidence?

It was minutes before I found my voice, but when I did, I tried to act nonchalant. "If you guys want to save your motel bill, I live a mile from here. There's a couch you could stay on tonight."

"That would be great," said Steve.

Far into the night I talked with Steve and his friend, Jim. I wanted to find out what had happened to Steve—did he still believe in God?

When I discovered he had a strong relationship with God and that his father's death had strengthened his faith, I grilled him mercilessly. Not once did I mention the book or my childhood. Instead, all of my questioning and anger spewed out toward Nate Saint's son. And he quietly answered each accusation with faith. The relief I felt at letting all of this out was enormous. After all these years, I could finally express my doubts, because Steve Saint had a God big enough and real enough to handle them.

The next day the weather cleared. I stood alone on the runway after Steve and Jim took off. Everything at Hunt's Airport was the same—except me. Twenty-four hours after that physical—and spiritual—storm, I knew that God had answered my prayer in the most personal, loving way possible. Again I had a joy inside that even an airplane had never been able to produce.

There's been a change in Linda's life, too; she also has a close relationship with Christ. We were married soon after Steve's visit, and since then have flown many missions to remote, impoverished villages in Mexico and Central America. But as long as I live, I'll never forget that November day after Steve Saint took off, when I gazed again into the sky—the sky my prayer had sailed through, the sky my dad and Nate Saint and I had flown through, the sky out of which that little Cessna had come barreling. And I knew that through that sky, over the horizon in Mexico and Central America, hungry villages waited for someone like Nate Saint—or me—to fly in with food, and a faith worth risking everything for. And, thanks to God, that faith again was mine.

Prayer

Lord, I know not what I ought to ask of Thee;
Thou only knowest what I need;
Thou lovest me better than I know how to love myself.
O Father, give to Thy child that which he knows
    not how to ask.

FRANÇOIS FÉNELON (1651–1715)

PRAYER THAT SUSTAINS

Along the Way

Though life's road is not a smooth one,
　　Opportunity still knocks:
God will show us how to fashion
　　Stepping-stones of stumbling blocks.

MILDRED N. HOYER

An Elevating Idea

SUSAN STETSON RENAULT

A while back, primarily for financial reasons, I needed to find a job outside the home. A job with a school seemed ideal, since it would allow me to be with my children in the afternoons and during school vacations.

I learned that a new high school would be opening in our district of Colorado Springs and decided that was where I wanted to work. I called the district office constantly—even before the new building was finished—asking for an interview. "For I know the plans I have for you," declares the Lord, "plans to prosper you and not to harm you, plans to give you hope and a future" (Jeremiah 29:11, NIV).

My prayers were answered, and I became a receptionist at the brand-new school. It took me about four days to discover that the job bored me to death. I grew exhausted reading newspapers. Wearily I'd watch the clock drag through the hours. I organized my paper clips twenty-one different ways.

One evening I collapsed onto the couch in despair. What could I do? "Then you will call upon me and come and pray to me, and I will listen to you" (Jeremiah 29:12, NIV). God *was* listening, and in His wisdom He reminded me of the elevator man.

Years before, when we lived in Chicago, we took some visitors to the Sears Tower. However, it wasn't the view from the world's tallest building that impressed me most. It was the elevator operator who whisked us up and down those 110 stories. He took a job that must certainly rank among the dullest in the world and made it fun. His friendly humor was contagious as he showed us how to bend our knees in preparation for landing. In a matter of seconds he made our lives a little brighter.

If this man could run an elevator joyfully, I could do the same with the reception desk. The trick was not to dwell on its dullness but to creatively introduce some fun into the job. It shouldn't be too hard, I thought. After all, how could a building with a thousand bright, fun-loving teenagers possibly be dull?

The next day I began a trivia contest by posting a provocative question beside my desk. No fanfare, no announcements—I just waited for students to notice. And when they did, I said, "A sucker for the right answer," having already stashed lollipops in my desk drawer. You'd think I'd offered a pot of gold. Kids raced to the library to learn the name of Australia's president.

My desk soon became a "stopping place," with students coming by first thing each day "to check the question."

I later put puzzles on my desk—a Rubik's Cube or peg-board teasers. During lunch hour or waiting to see an administrator, students would play with the puzzles or just talk to me. I became a sort of mother confessor—a friend.

And to anyone who inquired, "Doesn't your job get boring?" I'd say, "Not at all." And then I'd offer a prayer, thanking God for "elevating" me out of discouragement. Just as it says in Jeremiah 29:13 (NIV): "You will seek me and find me when you seek me with all your heart."

What to Pray For

Do not pray for easy lives.
Pray to be stronger men.
Do not pray for tasks equal to your powers.
Pray for powers equal to your tasks.

PHILLIPS BROOKS (1835–1893)

The Desperate Race

MARY JANE CHAMBERS

I opened the pages of The Washington *Post*—and stared. A gang of robber-rapists, the paper reported, was prowling the highways close to Washington, D.C., preying on women driving alone at night. The armed thugs would follow their victim on a lonely stretch of road, harassing her until she pulled over and stopped. Dozens of women had been victimized in the past month.

I looked at the story for a long time—but I already knew certain details all too well. My thoughts flashed back to the night two weeks before when I too drove alone—from Alexandria to Mount Vernon, on a five-mile stretch of the George Washington Parkway along the Potomac River.

I had attended a committee meeting at my church in Alexandria until about 9:00 p.m. When I got into my car to go home, out of habit I locked the doors. I was not especially concerned about driving home alone. After all, I'd been married for thirty years, had two grown sons. I'd led a protected life, really. Nobody had ever tried to harm me.

I drove two blocks down Belleview Avenue and swung onto the parkway. My husband and I often drove home from church this way on Sunday morning, when there were picnickers along the roadside and boaters on the Potomac. But now the recreation areas that bordered the road were deserted; there were no streetlights, and in the dark, the parkway, so busy during the day, seemed desolate. *I wish I hadn't come this way,* I thought.

Traffic was light. There were only a few cars in sight, all behind me. I stayed in the right lane while three of them passed me and sped off into the night.

A fourth car pulled up behind me. And stayed there. Apparently its driver was content to follow along at my speed. But the car did seem to be unusually close. I glanced in my rearview mirror, wondering if the driver realized how close he was to me. I guess he didn't.

Then the car drew even closer. Suddenly their headlights flashed, their *bright* lights. I gasped in surprise, quickly tilting up the mirror so I wouldn't be blinded by the glare. But their lights still lit up the interior of my car. Did they have some kind of spotlight?

Now I was worried. I had the strange feeling they were watching me intently. Why were they doing this? Were they kids out on a joyride? Whoever they were, this was a bad joke. And dangerous. "Dear God," I prayed, "make them pass me."

But if anything, they came closer. Bolder and bolder, they were now inches from my back bumper, their lights still trained on my head.

We went a mile, then two. They could see *me* clearly—but I couldn't see them. It seemed to me I'd seen two people in the front seat and another in the back. I wasn't sure. But now it was chillingly clear that these weren't just kids out on a lark. Whoever the dark figures in that car were, they were stalking me. I felt defenseless, and alone.

Near panic, I held tight to the steering wheel as though it could somehow take me out of this danger.

"Please, God," I prayed, "help me to know what to do."

Even before I finished speaking, I felt calmer. I unclenched my fingers and held the steering wheel more lightly. My shoulders relaxed, then my thoughts. And as my panic lessened, a voice sounded firmly in my mind.

Keep going. Don't stop.

But I couldn't stand those lights another minute. If I pulled over, they'd just pass me—wouldn't they? And the ordeal would be over.

You're on a four-lane highway that's practically deserted. They could pass you if they wanted to. Keep moving.

Like a student reviewing a problem in arithmetic, I thought of possible things I could do. I thought about turning off down one of the side roads. Again the inner voice:

You don't know this area very well. You could get lost. Or cornered.

I passed a sign that said, "Speed Limit 45, Radar Enforced."

If I speed up, I thought, *I may be able to attract the attention of the park police.* This time the inner voice was silent.

I pressed my foot on the accelerator and saw the speedometer zoom to seventy-five miles an hour.

For a few seconds I was free of the other car, but soon it was back at my bumper again. And no police car—or *any* car—appeared.

I went faster still, pulled ahead a bit, then slowed. So did they. The slower speed was even worse—torture in slow motion.

The feeling of fear took over again. My knuckles were white on the steering wheel. Again I was on the verge of stopping.

Is there something wrong with your car? said the inner voice.

I would have laughed if I hadn't been so frightened. My husband, a car fancier, faithfully kept our car running well.

Are you low on gas?

No, my husband just filled the tank.

Do you have a flat tire?

Obviously not.

This checklist cleared my head. I had no real reason to stop—and if I did I'd be putting myself in the hands of these strangers. I drove on.

Suddenly, to my own surprise, I began to sing. "Amazing Grace," "How Great Thou Art" and other hymns. My pursuers were flooding my car with glaring light. But I could flood it too—with God's strength and love. I sang as loudly as I could.

I was still trembling. But I was determined not to surrender. I began to think of how I could outwit my pursuers.

And you will think of something, the inner voice said. *God is with you.*

I was in familiar territory now, approaching the turnoff to the Mount Vernon highway that would take me to my neighborhood. As the intersection appeared, I pretended I was going to stop at the stop sign. At the last possible moment, I turned the wheel and stepped on the accelerator instead. My car careened around the corner, tires screeching. I raced down the highway like an Indianapolis Speedway driver.

My pursuers were thrown off—but only for a moment. They seemed to be fumbling with their gears, and by the time they recovered, I was almost a block ahead. Out of the reach of their glaring lights.

Again the inner voice spoke before fear could take hold. *Keep moving,* it said. *Don't stop. God is with you.*

Before my pursuers could catch up with me again, another car entered from a side street, inserting itself between us.

I turned off the highway onto Maryland Avenue, heading for home. In my rearview mirror I saw my pursuers turn too. But the other car had slowed them down and given me the lead I needed.

The road curved abruptly to the right—and there, momentarily concealed by the bend, was the entrance to my street! I swerved left again and raced toward my house. When I was barely a block away, I saw my tormentors shoot past behind me on Maryland, pursuing me in the wrong direction. From the way they were speeding, they would be blocks away before realizing they had lost me.

After following me down three different roads, they had missed the last turn! As I shut and locked the door of my home behind me, I almost cried with relief. Our house is on a cul-de-sac. If they hadn't missed that last turn they might have trapped me.

Now, two weeks later, as I looked at the newspaper account about these criminals, I felt horror—and yet a feeling of strength as well. "Aren't you terrified to go out at night now?" a friend had asked when I told her my story.

I'm definitely more cautious now. I always take sensible precautions when driving alone, especially after dark. But I'm not cowering in my house, living the life of a timid recluse. Fear didn't cause me to panic and pull over that night—and it's not going to stop me now.

I may drive down another dark road where terror and desperation await. Or I may find myself faced with some other emergency that seems hopeless. I know now that my hope and security reside in God, who guides me down every road and through every crisis.

Whatever comes, I will never have to face it alone.

Definition

Courage:
Fear that has said its prayers.

AUTHOR UNKNOWN

A Story of Answered Prayer

BRIGADIER GENERAL AND
MRS. JAMES L. DOZIER

G*eneral James L. Dozier:* My wife and I glance at each other.

Our apartment doorbell just rang; someone is outside in the hall. This is strange; visitors usually first ring the building-entrance bell downstairs.

As deputy chief of staff for logistics in a headquarters in the North Atlantic Treaty Organization's Southern Region, I have just returned from work to our apartment here in Verona, Italy. It is 5:30 p.m., December 17, 1981, and Judy is preparing dinner.

She touches my arm as I step toward the door. "I don't like it when the doorbell rings on our level," she says.

"I'm sure it's all right," I say, "probably one of the building people."

As I open the door it appears I'm right. Two bearded men in dark clothing politely explain they are plumbers. The smaller one carries a tool bag. Water, they say, is dripping into the apartment below and they need to find out if any of our fixtures is leaking.

I take them down the hall to the utility room where they seem to find everything in order. The bigger man uses an Italian word I don't understand so I go back to the kitchen and pick up my Italian-English dictionary. I'm suddenly jumped from the rear by one of the men.

Judy gasps as the other grabs her and we look into the muzzles of two pistols.

"We are the Red Brigades!" barks one of the men. The Red Brigades. The infamous terrorist group in Italy who have kidnapped and murdered numerous government and business leaders.

The smaller man pushes Judy to the floor while the large one and I continue to struggle. I fight, but pain explodes in my head from a blow and I crumple. I see Judy on her knees with a pistol pointed at her head and I stop fighting.

My arms are jerked behind me, steel handcuffs clamp my wrists; a gag is jammed into my jaws, and a cloth blinds me. Helpless, I hear the men let others into the apartment. Desk and bureau drawers clatter open and papers rustle as they ransack. I know they won't find anything confidential. But I worry about Judy and pray she won't be harmed.

Something sounding hollow and heavy is dragged up to me. Hands grasp me and I am stuffed into a large trunk.

I remember Aldo Moro, Italy's former prime minister, who was found dead in a car trunk fifty-four days after his kidnapping by the Red Brigades. The box lurches as I'm carried downstairs, and then it is slid onto a hard surface. A truck engine roars and we bounce over streets.

My chest begins to pound and I take small breaths to conserve oxygen. From time to time the lid flies back and cool fresh air pours in. Hands check my pulse; then the lid slams shut. They want to keep me alive, for the moment anyway. We rumble on and the trunk I'm in is transferred to what seems to be a car. Finally, we stop, and my trunk is lugged into a building. An elevator motor whines; controls click and buzz as we rise, drop and ascend. They are trying to disorient me. The door clangs open, I'm carried a short distance. The lid lifts; I am pulled out and lugged through what seems to be a small opening and dropped onto a cot. The gag and blindfold are removed and I sit blinking.

I'm inside a blue canvas cubicle about six feet square; it seems to be part of a tent erected inside an apartment. Three masked men chain my right wrist and left ankle to the metal cot. There is just enough slack in the shackles to reach a chemical toilet in a corner. This is my prison. For how long?

Mrs. James L. Dozier: I lie face down on the floor, ankles chained to wrists. I feel strangely calm. God must give this inner strength when we need it most. Just before the big man blindfolds me, I see a trunk by our kitchen door. I sense it is for Jim. Will I ever see him again? I pray for guidance to know when it will be safe to call for help.

A terrorist drags me down the hall to a room. I remain motionless while praying for Jim. Finally, the men leave. I dislodge the blindfold and look up into the blue flame of the water heater in our bathroom. Still chained wrist to ankle, I hunch along the tiles to the washing machine. I bang its metal side with my knees and call for help. But I do not know that our neighbors in the apartment below sit in the other end of their flat watching television. No one hears me.

Three hours have passed since Jim was taken. My knee is numb from thumping the washer, and my voice is dwindling to a croak. The doorbell rings; I call out again. Minutes later the glass crashes in a terrace window and the man who lives below rushes in crying, *"O mio Dio!"* Already his wife has phoned the police. Our neighbor's daughter had heard my calls when she had gone to the bathroom, which lies just below ours.

Gen. D.: Is Judy safe? It's all I can think of. My captors assure me that she is, and I sink back on the cot breathing thanks. I am not afraid of death; it has been a close companion for years, especially during combat. I know that death is only a transition into another life, a much better one promised by our Lord. But I am concerned for my family; we have a grown son and daughter and I don't want them to worry. I pray for them and everyone involved in this, that we maintain our proper perspective and be sensitive to God's guidance.

I survey my cell. In the outer section of the tent a masked guard sits, a call button taped to his chair arm. Another guard steps in and slips a stereo headset on my head. It is to prevent me from overhearing conversations. I am stunned by the high, piercing volume of hard rock music.

The din of shrieking crescendoes and exploding drums is excruciating. I have never cared for rock and roll and slump back onto the cot; the steel chains numb my wrist and ankle. How much longer can I stand this? I reach for the earphones but my guard is half out of his chair, sternly shaking his head no. Finally my mind turns off the noise.

The net. I gotta stay in the net.

Staying in the net is Army parlance for keeping in radio communication with your commander and fellow troops while out in the field. It is vital during battle; once you are out of the net, you are in trouble. My net with my Commander is maintained through prayer. Now more than ever I must keep in communication with my Commander. I learned this, long before my Army days, back in Arcadia, Florida. Dad died when I was fourteen, and Mom supported my sister and me there by teaching school. Only five feet tall, she was a spiritual powerhouse, continuing her teaching Sundays at the Methodist church. It was she who taught me to stay in the net. "God created you for a purpose, Jim," she said, "and the way to fulfill it is to keep in close touch with Him."

Keep in touch with Him. I set my mind on this. I see no human faces, only black masks. No matter what happens I know He will guide me and this whole affair will work out for the best. His will shall be done. A deep peace floods me and I fall asleep.

I awaken. They bring me toast and milk for breakfast. Now my inquisition begins. A terrorist squatting on the floor fires questions about NATO, my political beliefs.

I feel vulnerable. I do not want to discredit my country, Italy or NATO, and I pray for guidance. Then I feel a strange calm, as if I am in the company of others, other people who are praying for me, guiding me. *I'm trying hard to stay in the net.*

I answer the questions with harmless information. When we finish, they return my earphones. I ask for different music. One brings George Gershwin's *Rhapsody in Blue.* I sigh gratefully, but the volume is still high and my hearing is deteriorating.

I cannot tell time, either, as they took my watch. However, I find that when my guard is reading a magazine or talking with someone I can sneak the headset away from my ears an inch or so and hear sounds outside the building.

There are street noises, and I soon make out the typical traffic pattern of an Italian city. First, the morning rush hour, then the early afternoon *reposo,* with traffic picking up about 5:00 p.m., until the stores close at eight or so, and everything dropping off at midnight.

Now I can track passing days, and I attempt to follow a daily regimen, beginning and ending each day with push-ups, sit-ups and other exercises. I ask for a Bible and other books; they bring me only novels and news magazines. Perhaps they don't have an English Bible handy. I am grateful that I have read it through and remember some of it.

Mrs. D.: The Red Brigades have issued their first communique. It had been deposited in a trash container in Rome.
They call Jim a "NATO hangman" and say that he has been
taken to a "people's prison and will be submitted to proletar-
ian justice." They say they have declared war on the entire
NATO alliance as a "structure of military occupation."

Their fuzzy snapshot shows a bruise under Jim's left
eye. The police assure me that a massive search is on. All
that can possibly be done is being done.

Even in my sleep I think of Jim. My dream last night
was so vivid. It was as if we were talking. The strange thing
about it was Jim's hair; instead of his usual crew cut, it was
long and wavy. I know God sometimes speaks to us
through dreams. Is there some meaning in this? I don't
know and continue to pray for him.

Gen. D.: I feel a closeness with Judy as if she were with me.
I know she is praying for me; I sense it. After twenty-six
years of marriage there is a special relationship that distance and prisons cannot touch.

A week has passed since our separation and my face
itches from beard growth. The earphones' volume has been
lowered, but I'm tired of Gershwin. I have yet to see a
human face, only photos in old copies of *Time* and
Newsweek that my masked captors bring. They clip out the
stories they don't want me to see, but they did give me a
news photo of Judy; it becomes my pinup picture.

I pray for her peace of mind, for she knows my captors'
reputation for cold-blooded murder. In spite of my predica-

ment, I remain optimistic about the outcome. I am helped by something quite strong, a force supporting me like the lift one feels from an ocean wave, a powerful buoyancy.

I had the first feeling of this wave several days ago while I was doing pushups; a vivid impression came to me of my executive officer. He is a deep-thinking friend. I've always felt confident about bouncing my thoughts off of him. At first I wondered why I felt his presence so closely; then I knew. He was praying for me. I felt invigorated.

A few days later, while I was playing solitaire, I sensed the closeness of another friend. He teaches in the American school in Verona and is a gentle man who truly lives his faith.

It happened again yesterday afternoon; this time it was an American missionary who ministers to American service-men in Vicenza. I know now he is ministering to me.

And this morning while reading I found myself chuck-ling; it wasn't the book but a graphic impression of the feisty wife of a fellow general officer. She is an outspoken woman, and I can just imagine her calling Judy and saying, "Golly, as soon as I leave, things go to h— in a hand-bas-ket." She had left Europe shortly before I was kidnapped.

Now I know that not only Judy but all our friends—and other people—are praying for me. I know that all the resources of my country and Italy are at work endeavoring to free me. But nothing is more powerful than prayer. I long to thank these people who are praying for me, and I do so, in prayer.

Mrs. D.: Here in Verona, where my daughter and son have come to spend Christmas, the postmen bring packets of mail from Italians who write that they are praying for Jim. We also pick up more mail from Americans at our post office. They write of prayer chains and groups meeting on Jim's behalf.

It seems that prayers are rising for Jim around the clock everywhere. And friends are so supportive. The American and Italian communities have been such a help, and prayer groups are being organized worldwide.

The momentum appears to be building. I find myself smiling for the first time in weeks. What would we do without caring friends? I am also deeply touched by the many Italians who bashfully come to our door with flowers and gifts. So many say they are praying to Saint Anthony. "He is the one who finds anything missing," an elderly woman assures me. "I pray for him to find your husband. He will; you wait, you see."

It is Christmas Eve, 1981. As we return from chapel, I see the little candle in our window. It burns every night. It was a gift from a local mother whose little boy insisted that she buy it for "the general." As I light it, I am reminded of the prayers and love of people everywhere.

Gen. D.: From my reckoning I believe Christmas has passed. But my guards, who seem to know everything, told me about our son's and daughter's and my sister's arrival in

Verona. I'm grateful for that, but these chains are a nuisance. My unwashed body smells.

Mrs. D.: Jim has been reported dead. An anonymous caller told the police that he had been killed and hinted where his body could be found. The authorities are dragging a lake in the mountains. Can I keep my thoughts on God with such horrible news? But isn't this what Jim used to call "staying in the net"?

Gen. D.: The hoaxes I read about in news magazines regarding my death disturb me and I complain to my captors. They snort and say they "do not do tricks like that." I believe them. They play for keeps. But the waiting is tedious. A month has gone by; my beard is full and my hair long and wavy, not like the crew cut I have had all my life. But the chains...the chains are a nuisance. Wasn't there something in the Bible about Peter being in chains? I can't exactly remember. If Mom were here she'd know. Even after I graduated from West Point in 1956 and married Judy, Mom continued to send us copies of her weekly Sunday school lessons.

I smile in memory. When she was nearly sixty, she gave God what she called "an extra mile" by spending a year in India as a missionary. I lean back on the cot, my eyes moistening. Mom died just a year and a half ago but I can sense her presence. If she could do what she did, then I should be able to do whatever God expects of me right here, chains and all.

Mrs. D.: Six weeks have passed and the news isn't good. The authorities assure me that thousands of special investigators are searching for Jim. Yet to the press they express total frustration. "Dozier," said one top official, "could well be in the hands of the Martians, for all we know." Worse, the Red Brigades won't discuss Jim's release. "Negotiate? For what?" demands their latest communique. "The proletariat has nothing to negotiate with the bourgeoisie."

I have left Verona, first to visit friends in Naples and then on to Germany to stay with other close friends. I awaken this January morning feeling very optimistic. Why? I walk into the bathroom and look into the mirror wondering. All I know is that this is the day that the Lord has made and I should rejoice and be glad in it. But even when your husband has been a prisoner for forty-two days?

Gen. D.: I am starting to read the novel *1984* by George Orwell. It is not the most enjoyable story to read when a captive. "Big Brother" is all-pervasive. Yet I only have to remember the most powerful force of all, the love of our Father against whom the principalities and evils of this world are nothing.

My calculations tell me that I'm somewhere around my fortieth day of captivity. Jesus spent forty days alone in the desert. I guess we all have to wander through our own wilderness at some time or another. Yet, something strange has been happening. Lately, I have found myself playing a scenario in my mind over and over of what I will face on my release or rescue: the press conferences, debriefings. From where do such thoughts come?

There is a crash of splintering wood outside my tent, scuffling and shouts. My guard leaps to his feet and, with pistol aimed generally toward me, looks out the tent flap. A masked man bursts in and with one blow crumples him unconscious. Is it a rival gang invasion? My chains clattering, I grasp the masked invader, then feel the bulletproof vest under his black sweater. He hugs me and laughs. He is a commando from Italy's crack anti-terrorist unit. The locks on my two chains are released and they fall away; and I am escorted downstairs to a waiting car. They tell me that six thousand Italian investigators, working closely with the American and European experts, had conducted a mammoth sweep of suspects, following thousands of clues that led them to this apartment building in Padua, a town forty-eight miles east of Verona.

Thank God it is over.

Mrs. D.: I tell my friends how great I feel. We continue with our plans, and while preparing lunch, phone calls start to come in. Jim has been rescued! He's in good health and waiting for me in Italy. As our friends encircle me, cheering and crying, I stand in stunned silence. Our prayers have been answered—Jim is safe and coming home!

They say that Jim had been found in Padua. As with all Italian cities, it has a patron saint. The patron saint of Padua is Saint Anthony.

Gen. D.: Strange how the impressions given me in captivity have worked out in reality—the press conferences, the welcomes by the authorities and friends.

But, above all, one salient truth has been proven to me in a most amazing way. That our prayers for others, expressed in the love of God, can be our most powerful communication with them, transcending time and space.

For when I sat down with my executive officer, the American schoolteacher, the fellow general officer's wife, the American missionary and the many others whose loving, sustaining presences came to me in captivity so vividly, I learned in comparing notes with them that these happened at the very time they were earnestly praying for me.

"Who shall separate us from the love of Christ?" asks the Apostle Paul (Romans 8:35, 37). "Shall tribulation, or distress, or persecution, or famine, or nakedness, or peril, or sword?"

"Nay," is his ringing answer, for "in all these things we are more than conquerors through him that loved us!"

The Reasons Why

Not till the loom is silent,
And the shuttles cease to fly,
Shall God unfold the canvas,
And reveal the reasons why
The dark threads are as needful
In the Weaver's skillful hand
As the threads of gold and silver
In the pattern He has planned.

AUTHOR UNKNOWN

Prayer That Heals

At Even, When the Sun Was Set

At even, when the sun was set,
  The sick, O Lord, around Thee lay;
O in what divers pains they met!
  O with what joy they went away!

Once more 'tis eventide, and we,
  Oppressed with various ills draw near;
What if Thy form we cannot see,
  We know and feel Thou art here.

O Saviour Christ, our woes dispel:
  For some are sick, and some are sad,
And some have never loved Thee well,
  And some have lost the love they had;

  . . .

Thy touch has still its ancient power;
  No word from Thee can fruitless fall:
Hear in this solemn evening hour,
  And in Thy mercy heal us all.

HENRY TWELLS (1823–1900)

A Different Kind of Healing

VICTOR HERBERT

Guillain-Barré Syndrome is a rare and mysterious nerve illness named for the two French physicians who identified it. At its onset the patient feels a numbness in the muscles, followed by a paralysis that can advance rapidly through the body. If the lungs become totally disabled, the victim suffocates.

In 1962 I had a mild case of Guillain-Barré Syndrome. When I was back on my feet, the doctor warned me that it could recur. I was a busy young man with a wife, four kids and a great job as a sales engineer; it was easy to put that brush with GBS behind me. In fact, I forgot about it for two decades. Then came a summer morning in 1982 when I was a not-so-young-man of fifty-four.

I awakened to a strange tingling in the fingers of both hands. Like pins and needles. Then, as I swung my legs off the bed, I noticed that my thighs felt heavy. When I tried to stand, my knees buckled. I fell to the bed. I knew I'd felt that awful weakness once before.

By the time I was hospitalized that Friday afternoon, the weakness in my legs had become numbness. The next day, my belly and bowels became useless. My wife, Shirley, spent Saturday night in a chair in my room because I was unable to move from the waist down and felt the numbness moving up my chest. I was paralyzed.

On Sunday morning, while Shirley was at home changing clothes, the numbness started creeping into my lungs and throat. I was scared. I felt alone and helpless. In the dim, quiet hospital room I lay motionless, feeling something I had never felt before. A calling out from deep inside myself. A need that was as strong and real as hunger. I wanted God. I craved Him.

Years before, I'd left my faith behind when I left home for college. Science, I'd thought then, was a more reasonable source of answers to life than religion. Now, with my lungs turning to stone, I longed for God. Not only for the comfort of believing in Him. Even more, I wanted to feel I could entrust Shirley to His care. I needed to talk to Him about her.

As a child in a churchgoing family, I'd learned the Lord's Prayer. Now, groping for the old half-remembered phrases, I began to say it aloud. Though my voice was thin and rusty, the words sounded good to my ears. At the end I asked, "Please, Lord, take care of Shirley when I go."

Moments later I was gasping for breath. When I came to, I was in the Intensive Care Unit. Only my mind seemed to be functioning. It told me that I was as far removed from normal human life as a man could get. My body felt mummified. I was paralyzed from the chin down, bristling with plastic tubes that took care of my physical needs and dripped medicine into my veins. A respirator did my breathing for me. I couldn't move a muscle except for my eyelids. My field of vision was limited to a patch of ceiling and my communication consisted of spelling out words by blinking my eyes when someone pointed to letters on an alphabet card.

For two weeks the doctors worked on me, using an experimental treatment that involved exchanging my blood plasma for saline. Then the worst possible thing happened. I got pneumonia. And lost my last shred of humanity. My mind.

It happened this way. Hoping to protect me from further lung infection and from blood clots, the medical team decided to put me in a motorized bed that would keep my body in motion artificially. A Stryker frame, it was called. My body was held in place by a special covering to keep me from falling off as it turned me from side-to-side twenty-four hours a day, never stopping. It was like being lashed to the wing of an airplane that was banking steeply in a turn, first one way and then the other.

Very soon, my eyes began playing tricks on me. During the constant bizarre tipping and turning, my narrowed vision caught strange shadows. In the dim lights of the ICU, the tubes, bags and machinery took on eerie shapes. Shapes that moved menacingly. Shapes that became mad dogs, a pack of them milling viciously beneath my bed, snapping as my foot and hand dipped only inches from the floor, into their midst.

I was hallucinating, and I couldn't even cry out for help! Though I had been sending thought-prayers to God ever since my first awkward "Lord's Prayer," I now lost my mental grip on Him. Paranoia set in. The shadows of the men and women who tended my machines were those of torturers who were trying to kill me and make it look like an accident. I even spelled out M-U-R-D-E-R on the alphabet card with eye-blinks when Shirley held it up.

One day my family and the doctors and nurses spent hours convincing me that delirium from the pneumonia (which had collapsed one lung), lack of rest and my isolation were the problem. I believed them in the light of day, but that night, as shadows flickered on the walls and the "airplane" banked with me strapped to the wing, I slipped into delusion again. Into terror. *Lord,* I cried out in my mind, *keep me out of this hell. Please God! Show me how to stay with You.*

Briefly my bed twisted into a level position. A woman came into my sight line. A woman with reddish-gold hair and the saddest look on her face. I saw her only for a moment, and then the bed tilted away, down toward the other side, where the ugly shadows waited. Fiercely, I made myself concentrate on her to ward off the nightmare. I knew she was real because I'd glimpsed that reddish-gold hair in the daytime. She was the mother of a sixteen-year-old boy who'd been in the next cubicle—and he wasn't

expected to live, according to the low whispers of his
relatives.

I had never seen the boy, but his mother's face stayed
in my mind. A face anguished with despair for her son's life.
I knew despair. I'd felt it for my own life on the first Sunday
here. Suddenly I wanted to comfort that mother. But what
in the world could I do? Paralyzed, down with pneumonia,
pinned to a weird revolving bed, no voice, half out of my
mind....

I can't even help myself, I thought. *Only I* did *drag myself
out of despair that Sunday...when I prayed.*

At that moment I said another prayer. Involuntarily, in a
rush of compassion.

*O Lord, remember me? A sad, sad woman is here. Her
son is nearly dead. She's so scared. She held that boy in her
arms as a tiny baby fresh from You and as a little boy afraid
in the dark, and she wants to see him grow up. She's thinking
of all the little moments that mounted up to all this love she
feels. Please, Lord, keep her in Your loving care. Ease her
mind. Wrap that boy in Your healing Spirit. Save him, Lord.
I love him, too. I love her. ...*

An hour later, concentrating on prayer for the mother
and son, I was surprised to see that what had once been a
monstrous alligator was no more than my wastebasket with
a jagged package protruding from it. My panic was gone.

Night and day I prayed—and the hallucinations stayed
at bay. Gradually, the whispers of the boy's relatives were
less gloomy, and hope flickered in his mother's eyes. Then
the doctor said he *would* recover. I was still praying for this

boy I couldn't see, whose life had become infinitely precious to me, when a new patient came into the bed on the other side of me.

I could see the new occupant because his bed was hoisted high at an angle. All but his face was in a cast or bandaged. A motorcycle policeman, he'd been hit by a car while on duty. Immediately I began to pray for him, too. A wondrous feeling of strength swept through me with each prayer, as I concentrated on his bandaged limbs, one after another. Before long, the glow of God's healing seemed to spread over me and the equipment between our beds, and to pour right into the swathed figure. In time the policeman left the ICU, and eventually I learned that he was back on duty.

More time passed and I, too, left the Intensive Care Unit. And I recovered from Guillain-Barré Syndrome—a gift from God and a dedicated medical staff. Later I came across a Bible passage that summed up my experience and pointed the way to the future. "Keep sane and sober for your prayers. Above all hold unfailing your love for one another, since love covers a multitude of sins. Practice hospitality ungrudgingly to one another. As each has received a gift, employ it for one another" (1 Peter 4:7–10, RSV).

I believe that I kept sane *because* of my prayers for others. I had no idea that in helping them I'd be helping myself. I'll never forget that when I asked God to release me from my personal hell, He pointed me to the face of another human being.

How Does God Heal?

MICHELE STEGMAN

For many years my Grandmother Adams suffered from an excruciating pain in her jaw, and the doctors couldn't seem to help her. Grandmother lived in the Kentucky hills. She was a woman of strong faith, yet she did not pray for her healing.

Often she'd told me stories of how people, including my grandfather, had been cured by faith healers. One day when her pain seemed particularly intense, I said, "Didn't you tell me that James Wright can heal pains?"

"Yes," she nodded.

"Then go to him," I pressed.

"Oh, I'll see him at church sometime," she said in a tone that told me she would not.

Then it occurred to me that I had chided Grandmother for not praying for herself, yet never once had *I* prayed for her! Right then and there I began to ask God to heal her.

A few weeks later Grandmother found another doctor who thought he could help. She entered the hospital, received treatment and was cured. Her pain was gone.

Now I was disturbed again. *Well,* I thought, *faith and prayer hadn't healed Grandmother after all. The doctor had. God did not answer my prayer.*

Or had He?

Pals

PATRICIA BRADY

Although the McCurdy family lives around the corner from us, my son Jackie didn't really get to know Danny McCurdy until they started school. I guess it was my fault. Even though I truly like people, it's difficult for me to be the one who reaches out first. I'm always afraid I'll seem a little foolish.

Once Jackie and Danny did get acquainted, though, it became apparent to me that the bond of love between them was something special. I'd never seen anything like it in the friendships of my three older children. And I wasn't the only one who thought the boys' closeness rare. As the two little pals became a familiar sight in our neighborhood, more than one neighbor commented, "I never see those boys argue." And it was true. Whatever activity one suggested, the other agreed to.

Because of their physical appearances, it was easy to spot them at play. Jackie's blue eyes and blond hair contrasted sharply with Danny's brown eyes and straight dark hair. Unfortunately, there was a greater—though invisible—contrast between them. Jackie's excellent health was marred only by eczema on his legs, but Danny had lost a kidney to cancer before he started kindergarten.

When the boys turned seven, Danny's cancer recurred. This time part of his right lung was removed, and chemotherapy treatments were started. The treatments made Danny violently ill, and whenever I heard he was having a bad day, I had only to look at Jackie to confirm it. Jackie, who visited Danny whenever possible, would get so uptight he couldn't sit still, and he would scratch at his eczema more than ever.

Soon the chemotherapy caused all of Danny's hair to fall out. He tried to conceal his head by covering it with a red Phillies baseball cap. Whether Danny was sitting in class or at our supper table, the bright red cap clung to his head.

At first, I didn't realize why Jackie was badgering me for a cap exactly like Danny's. But as soon as he got it, Jackie placed the cap on his head the same way Danny wore it—with the brim turned toward the back. And, like Danny's, Jackie's cap stayed firmly in place from sunup to sundown. No amount of persuasion could convince him to take it off.

That July there was a special healing service at our parish church, and I had a growing feeling that Danny should attend it. There were to be several priests on hand to anoint the sick with oil. I asked Lorraine McCurdy,

Danny's mother, if my husband Jack and I could take Danny. She agreed to let him go.

When the evening of the mass arrived, Jack and I took our children and Danny to the church. It was hot and crowded inside. Perspiration began to darken the rims of the two red baseball caps and trickle down the boys' faces, but neither removed his cap.

Finally it was time for those seeking healing to go to the altar. "How about it, Danny?" I asked. " Do you want to go up and ask the Lord for a healing?"

"Nah," Danny said, his lashless brown eyes avoiding those of the people rising from their seats. "I'm sick and tired of being prayed over."

I knew, of course, that it was actually a case of "sick and tired of being stared at," something Danny had come to dread. Even though I understood that feeling only too well, I was upset by his answer. If anybody in that church needed a healing, it was Danny.

"What are we going to do?" I whispered frantically to Jack.

"I've got an idea that might work," Jack answered softly. Turning to Jackie, he said, " What about you, Jackie? Would you like to have prayers for your rash?"

I don't know what went through Jackie's mind as he pondered his father's question, but I know what raced through mine. *Do it for Danny, Jackie,* I pleaded silently. *Do it for Danny.*

"Okay," Jackie decided. "I'll get my rash prayed over."

My husband and I stood up and started to move forward. Our son slid from his seat and headed for the end of one of the lines. Danny, tugging at his cap, followed at his heels.

When we finally inched our way to the altar, we found that we'd been waiting in Father Curran's line. He was our parish priest and knew the boys' needs even better than they themselves did.

"Well, Jackie," he said. "What healing do you want from the Lord?"

"I want to get rid of this itchy rash, Father," he said, pointing to his bare legs.

Then Father Curran looked at Danny and his gaze softened. "And what about you, Danny? What do you want?"

Danny grinned shyly. "I'm not here for me, Father. I'm here for Jackie's rash."

Father Curran anointed the boys with oil and, placing a hand on each, began to pray. Jack and I, who were standing behind them, also laid our hands upon the children and prayed along with Father Curran. Jackie's rash practically forgotten, we silently begged God for Danny's life.

A few days later I was sitting on the beach at the lake, watching the two red caps bobbing about in the water. Jenny, a friend from church, joined me.

"Pat," she said joyously, "Danny's been healed."

My heart leaped. "How do you know?"

"I had a vision of Danny dashing into the lake. And you know what? He wasn't wearing his baseball cap. His hair had grown back in thick, black curls."

I wanted desperately to share Jenny's confidence, but something was wrong with that vision. Danny's hair had been straight. Yet soon after that, Lorraine McCurdy told me she could see hair starting to appear on Danny's scalp. And when it was finally in, we could all see for ourselves that it was thick—and curly.

When Danny returned to the hospital for his checkup, the doctors informed the McCurdys that Danny had responded to treatment. The cancer was arrested. The rejoicing in the Lord that took place in our parish was indescribable. In fact, my own gratitude to God was so overwhelming that weeks passed before I realized Jackie wasn't scratching at his eczema.

"Come here, Jackie," I said the afternoon it finally occurred to me. "Let me see your legs." He rolled up his jeans. The skin on his legs was clear.

Four years have passed* since the night of the healing service. Danny and Jackie, now eleven, are as close as ever and—except that Danny's hair has returned to its naturally straight state—are pretty much the same as the summer they were healed.

As if those of us who witnessed this miracle from God weren't blessed enough, He has heaped upon us His grace to overflowing. For no matter what the future holds for Danny and Jackie, the Lord has spoken to all of us through the love of two small boys. Hasn't he shown us firsthand how to become like children so that we, too, may enter the kingdom of Heaven?

*Written in 1982

As for me, I got a healing of my own. Now, whenever I find myself in a situation where I feel a little foolish reaching out, all I have to do is think back to the night of the healing mass and that desperately ill little boy who did not hesitate to step forward—no matter how "foolish" he may have felt—to help his friend.

Can I do less?

Healing the Hurt In Your Heart

VIRGINIA LIVELY

The woman kneeling at the altar rail was in pain—all of us taking part in the healing service could see that. Her face showed her intense agony.

"Migraine," the minister whispered to me as we moved toward her down the line of kneeling people.

Then I was standing in front of her. "I have migraine headaches," she explained. I laid my hands on her head and asked Jesus who loved her to take this pain away. Her mouth relaxed, and she opened her eyes like someone waked from a bad dream.

"It's gone!" she whispered.

"Thank You, Lord!" said the minister. "Thank You!" the congregation echoed. "Thank You" I repeated, most awestruck of all.

Although it was nine years since God had called me to His ministry of healing, I still could never get over the joyous surprise of it. My chief surprise was that He could use me—a middle-aged housewife with a spreading waistline and a kitchen in need of new linoleum—to reach out to people who hurt. But because it happened, over and over again, I'd stopped trying to figure it out and simply and gratefully gone ahead.

Why, then, as this now smiling woman went back to her pew, was I gripped with a strange uneasiness? A person had been in pain. The pain was gone. But all through the minister's closing prayers, I was puzzled.

Then I remembered something which was to shed light for me on the whole mystery of healing. I remembered that I had seen this lady before. It was right here in this same little Episcopal church the last time I'd been here, three years before. She had come forward with a blinding headache that night too. And God had healed her.

Then why was she back tonight? Was God's healing only temporary? Did it wear out and need renewing from time to time—like kitchen linoleum? Or was there something in this lady's life deeper than the migraine that needed healing? Something that lay behind the headaches and made them happen, something that she had never brought to the altar rail?

As people started up the aisle, I got to the woman's side and asked if she could stay behind. And so in a quiet pew we talked. When, I asked, had this last attack begun?

She thought a moment. "I guess it was just after Jeannie was so upset. She's our youngest, and you know how kids are. The older ones wouldn't let her into their clubhouse."

The more we talked, the more we saw a pattern. The headaches seemed to begin when she saw a child mistreated. A story in the paper, a church appeal for hungry orphans, one of her own youngsters up against life's small injustices, any of these could trigger an incapacitating attack that might send her to bed for days. And yet her own childhood, she said, had been unusually happy.

"My stepfather was a wonderful man. You see, mom wasn't married when she had me. But then she married my stepfather, and he raised me just like one of his own. We were a very religious family. Dad was superintendent of the Sunday school, and mom did the flowers, and I sang in the choir, funny as it seems."

"Why funny?"

"Because I—" The woman's eyes grew huge. " Because I can never go to heaven!"

She sat blinking in the dim-lit sanctuary. "I remember my stepfather saying it! He said he loved me and he'd give me everything he could here on earth but little girls like me could never go to heaven."

She had not thought of it with the conscious mind, perhaps, but beneath all the other thoughts of her life had lain this monstrous image of an unjust God.

Before we left the church that night, we went to the altar rail, just she and I, and held up to God this ugly, twisted picture of Himself. "Take it away, Father," I asked, "and show her Jesus instead." This is one reason why Jesus came, I told her, so we can know what God is really like. "Read the Gospels," I suggested. "Read them over and over until you have such a firsthand knowledge of Him."

That night, I know from subsequent letters, was the beginning of real healing for this woman. But it also marked a change in my own life. From that evening on, as people described the aches and pains which led them to seek God's divine healing power, I began listening for the deeper aches.

And I made an astonishing discovery. When we got down to the underlying problem, time after time, it was not medical, nor even, at its deepest, psychological. The real trouble was spiritual. And it was precisely the same problem—in a thousand forms—that the woman with the migraines had. These people had trouble loving God.

Some experience, some early training, some false concept, stood between them and true trust.

And there was the businessman who, deep down, did not want to be healed of his alcoholism. The drinking bouts, we began to notice, would start just when he was on the verge of some big sale or about to meet a potential customer. It turned out that he was the son of a pious but unsuccessful shoe salesman who had made a virtue of failure and taught that wealth is contrary to the will of God. My friend couldn't face success. He was afraid of his heavenly Father and didn't want to hurt his earthly father.

The more important a person's faith is to him, the more successfully he has usually hidden from himself this deep distrust of God. People will talk to me almost eagerly about the most agonizing physical condition or the saddest family relationship, but are tongue-tied when it comes to implicating God in these things.

I remember a minister who came to the house relating experiences of strangling attacks of asthma. His story was a familiar one of terror-filled nights and painful days.

When he had finished, I did not immediately begin to pray for healing as I once would have done. Instead I asked him to tell me about his very first asthma attack, and I prayed silently that Jesus would help him expose the real problem.

There was a long, long silence. Then haltingly he began to recall a hunting trip he had missed as a teenager. He was to have left in the morning with a friend and the friend's father, when he had waked in the night struggling for breath. "I wanted to go especially badly because I had no father of my own. You see, when I was nine my own father—my father—." And then this gray-haired man burst into tears. I have discovered that when the root problem is touched at last, there is usually anger or tears or both.

Chokingly the story came out. A well-meaning friend, trying to ease a little boy's grief, had explained to him that God had taken his father because He loved him and wanted him in heaven. And the little boy who loved and wanted his father too had grown up with an unacknowledged fury at a selfish God.

But now that the painful truth was out, we could pray for genuine healing, not just of the asthma but of the far deeper constriction at the very source of this man's life and health.

A portion of the prayer we offered together, which brought about the healing of that childhood memory of caprice and cruelty, may help others put to rest the deep hurts, fears and misunderstandings that trouble most of us.

"Jesus, we know that You are perfect love. But we confess that there are blind spots in our souls that hide this love from us. We ask for Your light in these dark places now, although we know that light can be painful. Burn away any false old images we have built and show us Yourself. Amen."

Immortal Love

Immortal Love, forever full,
Forever flowing free,
Forever shared, forever whole,
A never-ebbing sea!

We may not climb the heavenly steeps
To bring the Lord Christ down;
In vain we search the lowest deeps,
For Him no depths can drown.

But warm, sweet, tender, even yet
A present help is He;
And faith has still its Olivet
And love its Galilee.

The healing of His seamless dress
Is by our beds of pain;
We touch Him in life's throng and press,
And we are whole again.

JOHN GREENLEAF WHITTIER (1807–1892)

THE MERCY PRAYER

Lord Jesus Christ, have mercy on me.

A Short Form
MERYLL M. HESS

A friend told me that the Greek Orthodox have a prayer that goes "Lord Jesus, have mercy on me a miserable sinner." Someone realized that God already knew he was miserable, so he dropped that word, leaving "Lord Jesus, have mercy on me a sinner." Then he decided God certainly knew he was a sinner, so that was dropped. The editing continued until only one word was left: "Jesus!"

As a busy wife and mother of four, I have found many exciting uses for that prayer, while driving, cooking, answering children's questions. It adds hours of prayer to each hectic day.

The Mercy Prayer

CATHERINE MARSHALL

During a telephone chat, my friend Elaine was telling me about a christening she had just attended. "The baby being christened was not only crying but screaming," she said. "I could see how embarrassed the infant's parents were and I wanted to help them. So I prayed, 'Lord Jesus, have mercy on that baby and his father and mother.'

"Catherine, it was remarkable. The crying stopped immediately as if a faucet had been turned off."

I agreed that it was amazing, then added, "But, Elaine, the result doesn't surprise me as much as your particular petition."

"How so?"

"Oh, just that the 'have mercy' seems such an extreme request in a relatively mild situation. Most of us think of mercy as connected with a dire emergency. The word conjures up a mental picture of a condemned man standing before a judge pleading for pity."

Then Elaine explained how it had indeed been a dire emergency that had begun to reveal to her the many facets of God's mercy ...

Eight years before, her husband Louis had undergone a serious cancer operation. He recovered and had been in good health until last summer when his doctor suspected a return of the cancer. "It was a time of great agony," Elaine told me. "All my reading of Scripture and praying—hours of it—led to a fresh realization of the unceasing compassion of a God of love.

"So my praying," she went on, "finally jelled into a single, heartfelt plea, 'Father in Heaven, will You have mercy on us simply for Jesus' sake?' "

The result? The cancer scare proved to be a false alarm.

But then Elaine went on to explain that, since then, God keeps showing her how He wants us to ask for and accept His mercy even in everyday things.

In the next few days, it was remarkable how passage after passage of Scripture verifying Elaine's Mercy Prayer was brought to my attention. I saw that many of Jesus' healings came as the result of a plea for mercy.

For instance, there were the two blind men sitting by the side of the road as Jesus was leaving Jericho (Matthew 20: 29–34). Hearing that this was Jesus passing by, the two men cried out, "Have mercy on us, O Lord, thou son of David."

The crowd following the Master told them to keep quiet. But the blind men cried the louder, "Have mercy on us."

And Jesus, standing still and giving the men His full attention, asked what they wanted of Him. When they begged Jesus to open their eyes, *He had compassion on them,* touched the eyes of both men, and immediately each received his sight.

Then there was the time Jesus met ten lepers (Luke 17:11–19). Since lepers were ostracized from public gatherings, these men stood at a distance, crying, "Jesus, Master, have mercy on us."

The Master did not question each man about how well he had kept the Law or how righteous he was. Simply out of Jesus' overflowing, compassionate love, He healed them. "Go and show yourselves to the priests," He told them. And later, "Your faith has restored you to health" (The Amplified Bible).

Faith in what or in whom? The connecting link is our belief that God loves each of us with a love more wondrous than the most warmhearted person we know; that He heals simply out of His love and because He wants us to have the joy of abundant health. As the Apostle Paul put it: "Blessed be the God and Father of our Lord Jesus Christ, the Father of mercies and God of all comfort, who comforts us in all our affliction" (2 Corinthians 1:3, 4, RSV).

In another place Paul tells us why Jesus did not inquire about the worthiness of those whom He healed or lifted out of sin: "So then (God's gift) is not a question of human will and human effort, but of God's mercy ..." (Romans 9:16, Amplified). In other words, there is nothing you or I can do to earn God's gifts. We are dependent on His loving mercy.

When I searched out the word *mercy* in Cruden's *Concordance,* I found a surprisingly long list of Scripture references. Moreover, Alexander Cruden's original words of description set down in 1769 are rich food for thought: "Mercy signifies that essential perfection in God, whereby He pities and relieves the miseries of His creatures"; and " 'Grace' flows from 'mercy' as its fountain."

The insights about the Mercy Prayer were not over yet. During a wakeful time in the middle of the next night, the inner Voice (there is no mistaking it!) forcibly reminded me of the particular words of the promise God had given me on the morning of Peter Marshall's death back in 1949. It had come as I had been about to leave the hospital room in which my husband's body lay. Even as I had reached for the doorknob, it was as if a firm hand had stopped me. Then, clearly and emphatically, yet with tenderness combined with surprising power, had come, "Goodness and mercy shall follow you all the days of your life."

And now, so many years later, deep in the night, the same Voice was saying, "Note that word 'mercy,' Catherine. *My* goodness, *My* mercy. That's what is following you and will surround you to the end of your earthly walk. Lean back on that. Depend on it."

How needed that assurance was for me at a particular moment thirty-three years ago. How needed for anyone in distress!

For who among us does not have needs in our troubled age? And to meet those needs, the resounding validity of the Mercy Prayer all through Scripture is meant for every one of us ... "The Lord is good; his *mercy* is everlasting; and his truth endureth to all generations" (Psalm 100:5, *italics added*).

Prayer

O Lord,
support us all the day long,
until the shadows lengthen and the evening comes,
and the busy world is hushed.
Then in Thy mercy grant us a safe lodging,
and a holy rest,
and peace at the last.

BOOK OF COMMON PRAYER, 1928